#1 Teacher Recommended!

BRIDGING GRADES
K to 1

Carson Dellosa Education
Greensboro, North Carolina

Caution: Exercise activities may require adult supervision. Before beginning any exercise activity, consult a physician. Written parental permission is suggested for those using this book in group situations. Children should always warm up prior to beginning any exercise activity and should stop immediately if they feel any discomfort during exercise.

Caution: Before beginning any food activity, ask parents' permission and inquire about the child's food allergies and religious or other food restrictions.

Caution: Nature activities may require adult supervision. Before beginning any nature activity, ask parents' permission and inquire about the child's plant and animal allergies. Remind the child not to touch plants or animals during the activity without adult supervision.

Caution: Before completing any balloon activity, ask parents' permission and inquire about possible latex allergies. Also, remember that uninflated or popped balloons may present a choking hazard.

The authors and publisher are not responsible or liable for any injury that may result from performing the exercises or activities in this book.

Summer Bridge®
An imprint of Carson Dellosa Education
PO Box 35665
Greensboro, NC 27425 USA

© 2015 Carson Dellosa Education. Except as permitted under the United States Copyright Act, no part of this publication may be reproduced, stored, or distributed in any form or by any means (mechanically, electronically, recording, etc.) without the prior written consent of Carson Dellosa Education.

Printed in Ningbo, Zhejiang, China • All rights reserved.   ISBN 978-1-4838-1580-0

01-0202512936

Table of Contents

Making the Most of *Summer Bridge Activities*®...iv
Skills Matrix vi
Summer Reading for Everyone viii
Summer Learning Is Everywhere! x

Section I: Monthly Goals and Word List 1

Introduction to Flexibility..2
Activity Pages 3
Science Experiments..43
Social Studies Activities 45
Outdoor Extension Activities..48

Section II: Monthly Goals and Word List 49

Introduction to Strength...50
Activity Pages 51
Science Experiments and Activity 91
Social Studies Activities 94
Outdoor Extension Activities..96

Section III: Monthly Goals and Word List 97

Introduction to Endurance...98
Activity Pages 99
Science Experiments..139
Social Studies Activities 141
Outdoor Extension Activities..144

Answer Key...145
Flash Cards
Certificate of Completion

Making the Most of *Summer Bridge Activities*®

This book will help your child review kindergarten skills and preview first grade skills. Inside, find lots of resources that encourage your child to practice, learn, and grow while getting a head start on the new school year.

Just 15 Minutes a Day
...is all it takes to stay sharp with learning activities for each weekday, all summer long!

Month-by-Month Organization
Three color-coded sections match the three months of summer vacation. Each month begins with a goal-setting and vocabulary-building activity. You'll also find an introduction to the section's fitness and character-building focus.

Daily Activities
Two pages of activities are provided for each weekday. They'll take about 15 minutes to complete. Activities cover math, reading comprehension, writing, grammar, and more.

Special Features

FITNESS FLASH: Quick exercises to develop strength, flexibility, and fitness

CHARACTER CHECK: Ideas for developing kindness, honesty, tolerance, and more

FACTOID: Fun trivia facts

© Carson Dellosa Education

Plenty of Bonus Features
...match your child's needs and interests!

Bonus Activities
Social studies activities explore places, maps, and more—a perfect complement to summer travel. Science experiments invite your child to interact with the world and build critical thinking skills.

Take It Outside!
A collection of fun ideas for outdoor observation, exploration, learning, and play is provided for each summer month.

Skill-Building Flash Cards
Cut out the cards at the back of the book. Store in a zip-top bag or punch a hole in each one and thread on a ring. Take the cards along with you for practice on the go.

Give a High-Five
...to your child for a job well done!

Star Stickers
Use the star stickers at the back of the book. Place a sticker in the space provided at the end of each day's learning activities when the pages are complete.

Praise and Rewards
After completing learning activities for a whole week or month, offer a reward. It could be a special treat, an outing, or time spent together. Praise the progress your child has made.

Certificate of Congratulations
At the end of the summer, complete and present the certificate at the back of the book. Congratulate your child for being well prepared for the next school year.

Skills Matrix

Day	Addition	Alphabet	Character Development	Classification	Fitness	Geometry & Measurement	Grammar & Language Arts	Graphing & Probability	Handwriting	Numbers & Counting	Phonics	Reading Comprehension	Science	Shape Recognition	Social Studies	Subtraction	Time & Money	Visual Discrimination
1		★				★												
2									★		★							
3									★		★			★				
4									★	★	★							
5	★				★				★		★					★		
6		★							★	★	★							
7		★							★	★	★							
8									★	★	★				★			
9		★							★	★	★							
10		★							★		★							
11				★				★	★		★							
12	★								★		★					★		
13							★		★	★	★							
14						★			★		★							
15					★				★	★	★							
16									★	★	★							
17							★		★		★							
18									★	★	★							
19									★		★							
20			★					★	★		★							
BONUS PAGES!			★	★									★		★			★
1	★								★		★	★						
2	★			★					★		★							
3	★							★	★		★							
4							★			★	★							
5			★							★	★	★						
6							★		★		★					★		
7							★				★					★		
8										★	★					★	★	
9						★			★		★					★		
10	★										★					★		★
11									★	★	★			★				

Skills Matrix

Day	Addition	Alphabet	Character Development	Classification	Fitness	Geometry & Measurement	Grammar & Language Arts	Graphing & Probability	Handwriting	Numbers & Counting	Phonics	Reading Comprehension	Science	Shape Recognition	Social Studies	Subtraction	Time & Money	Visual Discrimination
12	★					★					★					★		
13	★					★					★	★				★		
14	★								★	★	★					★		
15							★				★							
16						★	★				★							
17				★			★				★							
18											★	★		★				
19							★			★								
20				★			★			★							★	
Bonus				★			★		BONUS PAGES!				★		★			★
1	★						★			★						★		
2							★			★	★							
3				★							★	★						
4	★										★			★				
5							★				★							
6	★										★					★		★
7											★					★	★	
8	★						★				★							
9	★					★					★							
10							★				★					★		
11							★				★							
12	★										★	★				★		
13							★			★	★							
14	★										★					★		
15	★		★													★		
16	★						★									★		
17						★					★							
18	★						★					★						
19				★			★				★						★	
20						★					★							
Bonus				★			★		BONUS PAGES!				★		★			

Summer Reading for Everyone

Reading is the single most important skill for school success. Experts recommend that kindergarten and first grade students read for at least 15 minutes each day. Help your child choose several books from this list based on his or her interests. Choose at least one fiction (F) and one nonfiction (NF) title. Then, head to the local library to begin your reading adventure!

If you like poems...
Bringing the Rain to Kapiti Plain
   by Verna Aardema (F)
Did You Hear What I Heard?
   by Kay Winters (NF)

If you like stories about jobs...
When I Grow up
   by Al Yankovic (F)
I Want to Be a Doctor
   by Laura Driscoll (NF)

If you like animals...
Slinky Malinki, Open the Door
   by Lynley Dodd (F)
Finding Winnie: The True Story of the World's Most Famous Bear
   by Lindsay Mattick (NF)

If you like sports...
Jabari Jumps
   by Gaia Cornwall (F)
Brothers at Bat: The True Story of an Amazing All-Brother Baseball Team
   by Audrey Vernick (NF)

If you like space...
Voyage to the Bunny Planet
by Rosemary Wells (F)
Mae Among the Stars
by Rhoda Amed (NF)

If you like art...
Splatter
by Diane Alber (F)
Touch the Art: Feed Matisse's Fish by Julie Appel and Amy Gugliemo (NF)

If you like music...
Pete the Cat: Rocking in My School Shoes
by Eric Litwin (F)
Zin! Zin! Zin! A Violin
by Lloyd Moss (NF)

If you like science...
If I Built a Car
by Chris Van Dusen (F)
Here We Are: Notes for Living on Planet Earth
by Oliver Jones (NF)

If you like stories about the past...
King Bidgood's in the Bathtub
by Audrey Wood (F)
Locomotive
by Brian Floca (NF)

If you like stories about friendship...
One
by Kathryn Otoshi (F)
Tarra & Bella: The Elephant and Dog Who Became Best Friends
by Carol Buckley (NF)

Summer Learning Is Everywhere!

Find learning opportunities wherever you go, all summer long!

Reading

- Make a list of your top three favorite books. Check in at the beginning of each month to see if it has changed.
- Read signs, recipes, maps, weather reports, news articles, and other nonfiction texts that provide useful information.

Language Arts

- Trade letters, emails, or texts with a friend or relative to share summer adventures. Include stories, poems, facts, drawings, and photos.
- Make up a song about one of your favorite memories or a trip you might like to take.

Math

- Practice addition and subtraction with common items. Try subtracting grapes as you eat a healthy snack!
- Make a math obstacle course. Jump on sidewalk-chalked numbers, divide rocks into piles, do a number of jumping jacks to solve a problem, or meet other challenges.

Science & Social Studies

- Learn about stars, the Milky Way, meteors, the moon, and other things in space. Set up blankets under the night sky and invite friends. Teach what you learned.
- Spend time with a grandparent or another older person. Teach them a game, song, or dance you like. Ask them to teach you a game, song, or dance from when they were your age.

Character & Fitness

- Work with an adult to make a list of goals you have for the summer. Include things like counting to a certain number or drawing your favorite animal. Think about what you might need to complete those goals.
- Learn how to use a new physical skill. It could be skipping rope, throwing a baseball, or even doing a new dance. Keep trying until you feel confident.

© Carson Dellosa Education

SECTION 1

Monthly Goals

A *goal* is something that you want to accomplish. Sometimes, reaching a goal can be hard work!

Think of three goals to set for yourself this month. For example, you may want to exercise for 10 minutes each day. Have an adult help you write your goals on the lines.

Place a sticker next to each of your goals that you complete. Feel proud that you have met your goals!

1. _____ PLACE STICKER HERE

2. _____ PLACE STICKER HERE

3. _____ PLACE STICKER HERE

Word List

The following words are used in this section. They are good words for you to know. Read each word aloud with an adult. When you see a word from this list on a page, circle it with your favorite color of crayon.

animal	number
color	past
lowercase	set
more	shape
noun	uppercase

SECTION 1

Introduction to Flexibility

This section includes fitness and character development activities that focus on flexibility. These activities are designed to get your child moving and to get her thinking about building her physical fitness and her character. If your child has limited mobility, feel free to modify any suggested exercises to fit individual abilities.

Physical Flexibility

Flexibility, to the average person, means being able to accomplish everyday physical tasks easily, like bending to tie a shoe. These everyday tasks can be difficult for people whose muscles and joints have not been used and stretched regularly.

Proper stretching allows muscles and joints to move through their full range of motion, which is key to maintaining good flexibility. There are many ways that your child stretches every day without realizing it. She may reach for a dropped pencil or a box of cereal on the top shelf. Point out these examples to your child and explain why good flexibility is important to her health and growth. Challenge her to improve her flexibility consciously. Encourage her to set a stretching goal for the summer, such as practicing daily until she can touch her toes.

Flexibility of Character

While it is important to have a flexible body, it is also important to be mentally flexible. Share with your child that being mentally flexible means being open minded. Talk about how disappointing it can be when things do not go her way and explain that disappointment is a normal reaction. Give a recent example of when unforeseen circumstances ruined her plans, such as having a trip to the park canceled because of rain. Explain that there will be situations in life when unexpected things happen. Often, it is how a person reacts to those circumstances that affects the outcome. By using relatable examples, you can arm your child with tools to be flexible, such as having realistic expectations, brainstorming solutions to make a disappointing situation better, and looking for good things that may have resulted from the initial disappointment.

Mental flexibility can take many forms. For example, respecting the differences of other children, sharing, and taking turns are ways that your child can practice flexibility. Encourage your child to be flexible and praise her when you see her exhibiting this important character trait.

Measurement

DAY 1

Track your growth this summer. Have an adult help you measure your height. Fill in the blank. Draw and color the picture to look like you.

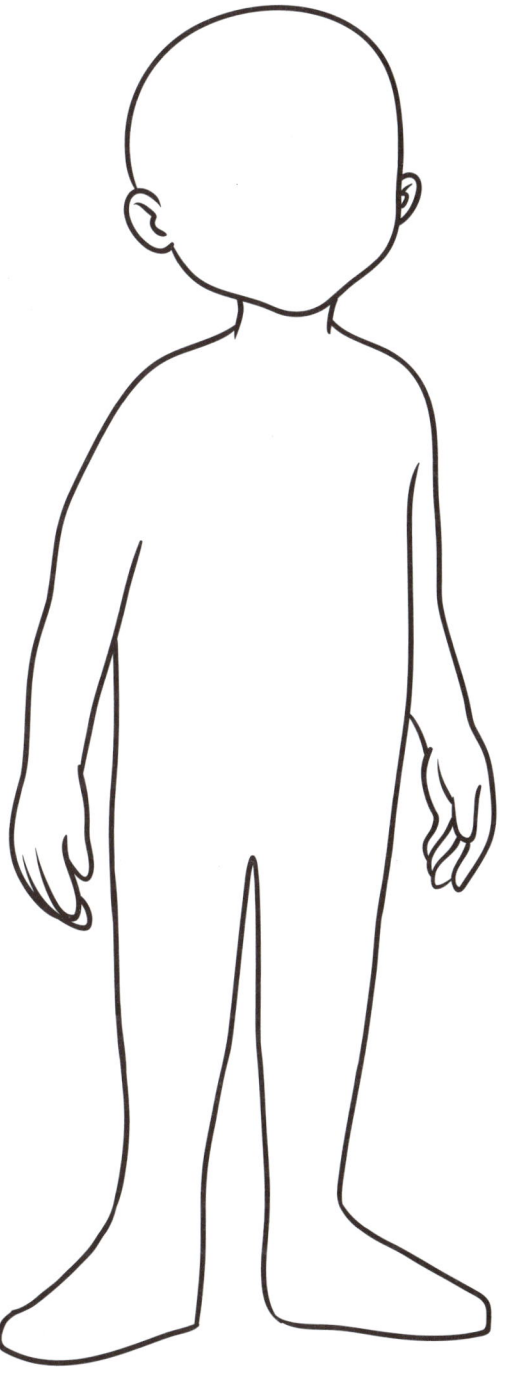

Your Height:

_____

DAY 1

Alphabet

Say the alphabet in order. Touch each letter as you say it.

Aa	Bb	Cc	Dd
Ee	Ff	Gg	Hh
Ii	Jj	Kk	Ll
Mm	Nn	Oo	Pp
Qq	Rr	Ss	Tt
Uu	Vv	Ww	Xx
Yy	Zz		

Ask an adult to say a letter. Find the letter and put a marker on it. Keep going until you have covered every letter.

Handwriting/Phonics

DAY 2

Trace and write the numbers 0–7.

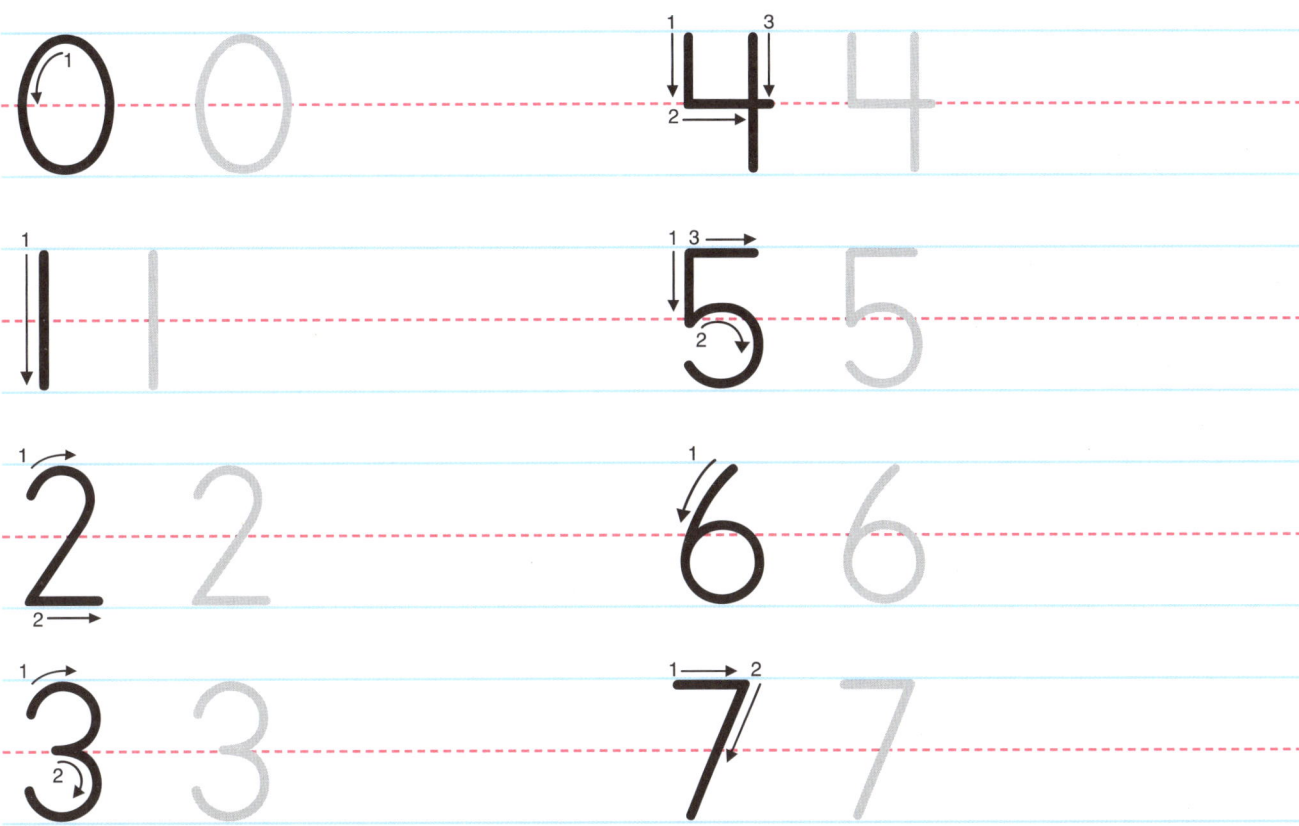

Read each word. Circle the pictures in each row that rhyme with the word.

1. cat
2. fan
3. hop

DAY 2

Handwriting/Phonics

Baseball begins with the /b/ sound. Practice writing uppercase and lowercase **B**s.

Say the name of each picture. Circle each picture that begins with the /b/ sound, like *baseball*.

FACTOID: Most baseballs have 108 stitches.

Handwriting/Shape Recognition

DAY 3

Trace and write the numbers 8–15.

8 8   12 12

9 9   13 13

10 10   14 14

11 11   15 15

Name each shape below. Circle the flat shapes. Underline the solid shapes.

DAY 3

Handwriting/Phonics

Cake begins with the hard *c* sound. Practice writing uppercase and lowercase *C*s.

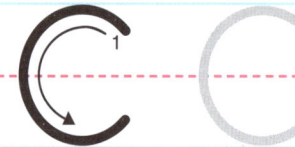

Say the name of each picture. Circle each picture that begins with the hard *c* sound, like *cake*.

 **FITNESS FLASH:** Touch your toes 10 times.

* See page ii.

8

© Carson Dellosa Education

Handwriting/Numbers & Counting

DAY 4

Trace and write the numbers 16–20.

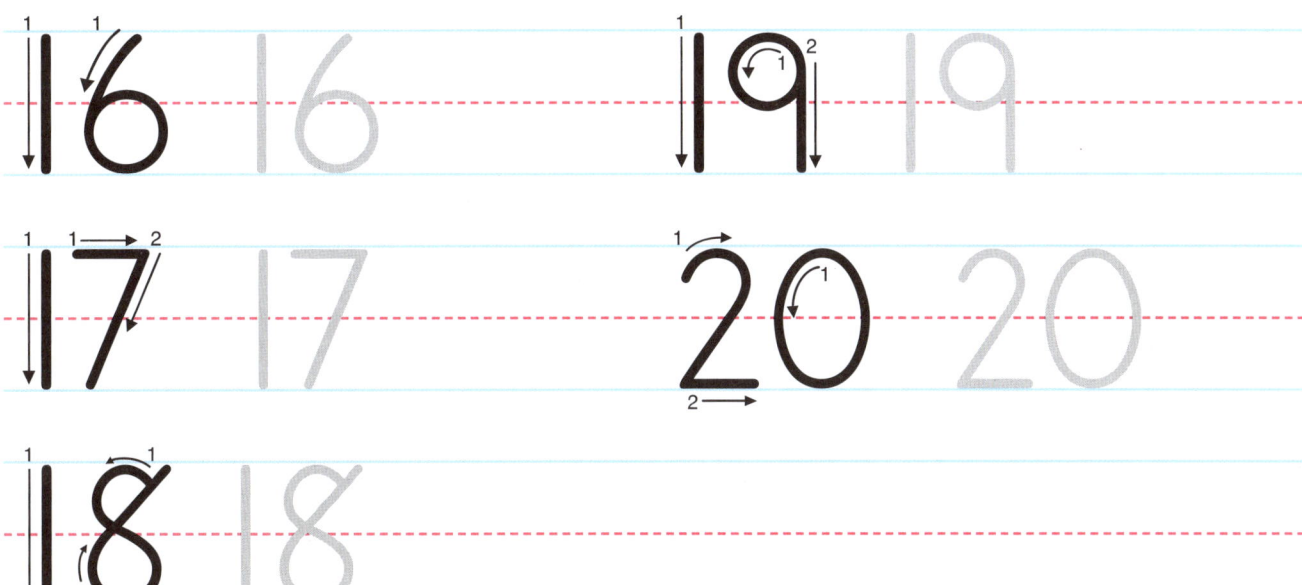

Write the next number in each set.

1. | 7 | 8 | |

2. | 2 | 3 | |

3. | 14 | 15 | |

4. | 18 | 19 | |

DAY 4

Handwriting/Phonics

Duck begins with the /d/ sound. Practice writing uppercase and lowercase **D**s.

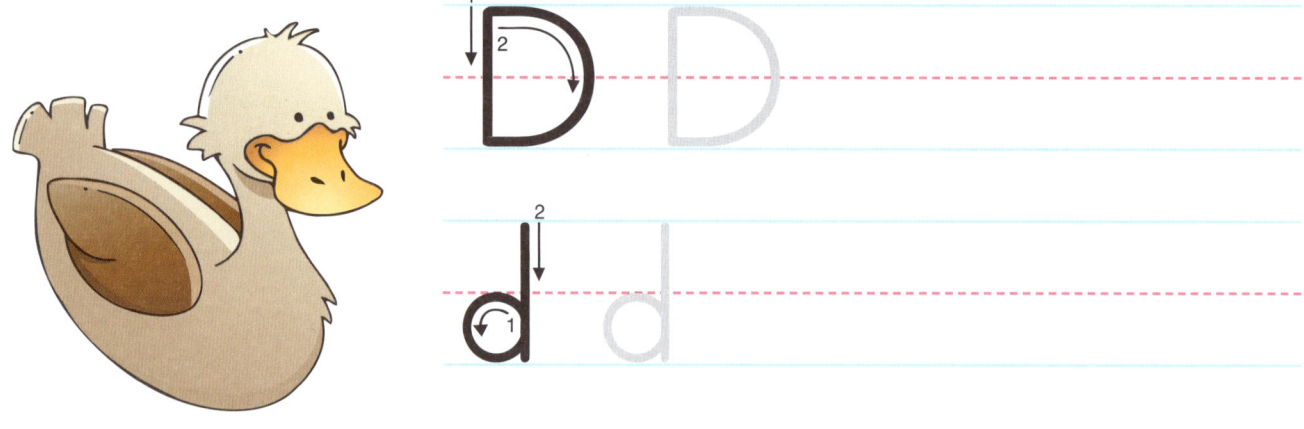

Say the name of each picture. Circle each picture that begins with the /d/ sound, like *duck*.

FACTOID: Ducks stay dry in the water because their feathers are waterproof.

Addition & Subtraction/Fitness

DAY 5

Count the frogs in the pond. Write an addition or subtraction sentence to help you answer each question.

1. How many frogs are in the pond? _____

2. How many frogs will be in the pond if 3 frogs hop away?

   _____

3. How many frogs will be in the pond if 6 frogs hop away?

   _____

4. If 4 new frogs hop into the pond, how many will there be?

   _____

Animal Stretch

Choose your favorite animal. Imagine how the animal stretches. Practice stretching like the animal. Then, show your family and friends. Can they guess the animal that you chose?

* See page ii.

DAY 5

Handwriting/Phonics

Fish begins with the /f/ sound. Practice writing uppercase and lowercase **F**s.

Say the name of each picture. Circle each picture that begins with the /f/ sound, like *fish*.

 **FITNESS FLASH:** Practice a V-sit. Stretch three times.

* See page ii.

Numbers & Counting/Alphabet

DAY 6

Say each number. Color the number of boxes to match the number. How many more boxes would you need to color to make 10?

6										
7										
8										
9										
10										

Write the missing lowercase letters.

a, b, ___, ___, e, ___, g, ___, i, ___,

k, ___, ___, n, o, ___, q, ___,

___, ___, u, v, ___, ___, ___, z

DAY 6

Handwriting/Phonics

Girl begins with the hard *g* sound. Practice writing uppercase and lowercase **G**s.

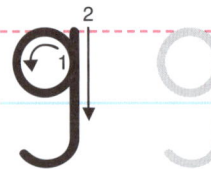

Say the name of each picture. Circle each picture that begins with the hard *g* sound, like *girl*.

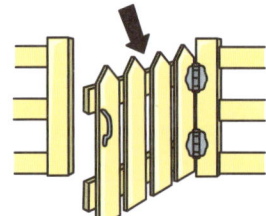

CHARACTER CHECK: With an adult, look up the word *caring* in the dictionary. Talk about a time when you were caring.

Numbers & Counting/Alphabet

DAY 7

Count the number of objects in each set. Write the number on the line.

1.
_____

2.
_____

3.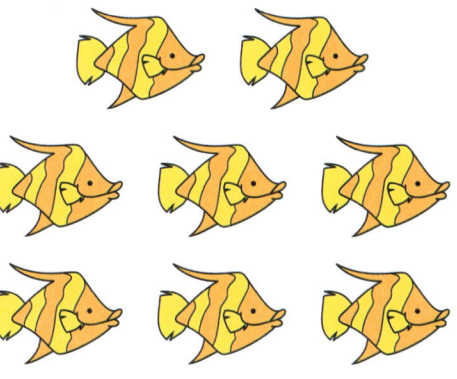
_____

4.
_____

Write the missing uppercase letters.

A, B, ___, ___, E, ___, ___, H, ___,

___, ___, ___, M, ___, ___, ___, Q,

___, S, ___, ___, ___, W, ___, ___, Z

DAY 7

Handwriting/Phonics

Horse begins with the /h/ sound. Practice writing uppercase and lowercase Hs.

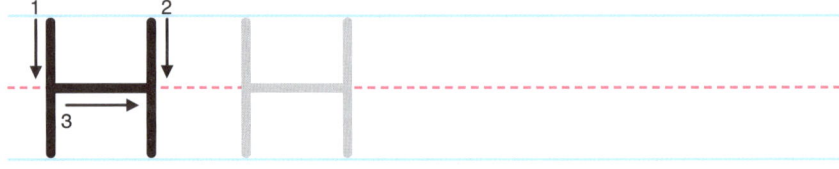

Say the name of each picture. Circle each picture that begins with the /h/ sound, like *horse*.

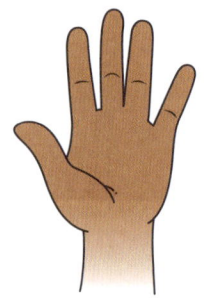

FACTOID: A horse cannot see what is directly in front of its face.

Shape Recognition/Numbers & Counting

DAY 8

Draw the correct number of shapes in each box.

1.

2.

8 circles

4 rectangles

3.

4.

5 squares

7 ovals

Count each set of blocks. Write the number.

5.

_____

6.

_____

7.

_____

8.

_____

9.

_____

10.

_____

DAY 8

Handwriting/Phonics

Jack-in-the-box begins with the /j/ sound. Practice writing uppercase and lowercase **J**s.

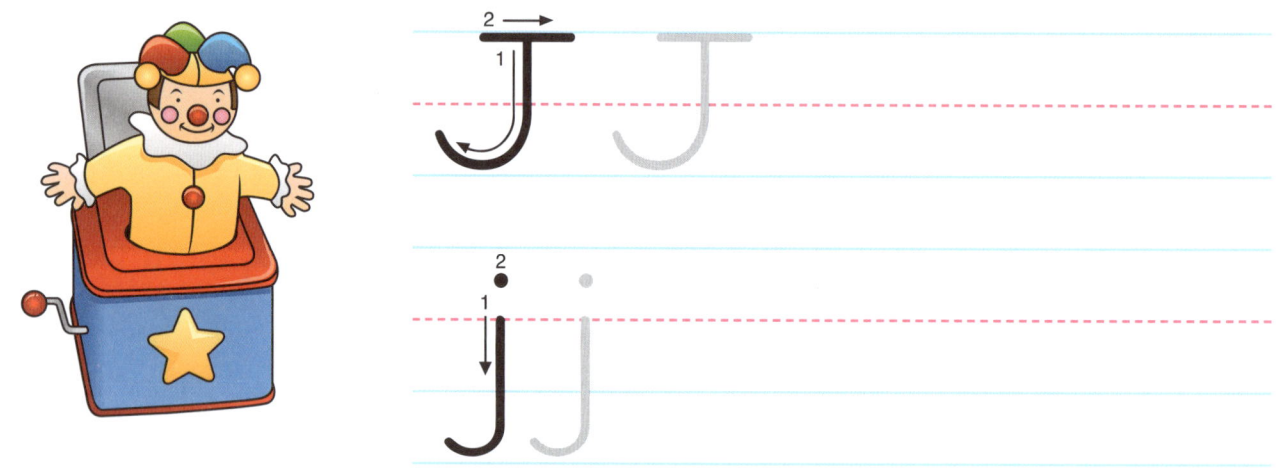

Say the name of each picture. Circle each picture that begins with the /j/ sound, like *jack-in-the-box*.

   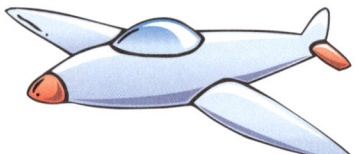   

 **FITNESS FLASH:** Do 10 shoulder shrugs.

* See page ii.

Numbers & Counting / Alphabet

DAY 9

Circle the number in each set that is more.

EXAMPLE:

	1.	2.
(8) or 5	7 or 1	9 or 6
3. 4 or 0	4. 2 or 10	5. 8 or 7

Circle the number in each set that is less.

EXAMPLE:

	6.	7.
5 or (3)	10 or 0	2 or 5
8. 1 or 11	9. 0 or 10	10. 4 or 9

Draw a line to match each uppercase letter to its lowercase letter.

A   c   G   g

B   a   H   l

C   f   I   j

D   d   J   h

E   e   K   i

F   b   L   k

DAY 9

Handwriting/Phonics

Kangaroo begins with the /k/ sound. Practice writing uppercase and lowercase **K**s.

Say the name of each picture. Circle each picture that begins with the /k/ sound, like *kangaroo*.

FACTOID: A baby kangaroo is called a *joey*.

Phonics/Alphabet

DAY 10

Say the name of each picture. Circle the number that tells how many syllables are in each word.

1.
   1   2

2.
   1   2

3.
   1   2

Draw a line to match each uppercase letter to its lowercase letter.

M	p	T	u
N	m	U	t
O	q	V	v
P	r	W	x
Q	s	X	z
R	n	Y	y
S	o	Z	w

DAY 10

Handwriting/Phonics

Ladybug begins with the /l/ sound. Practice writing uppercase and lowercase **L**s.

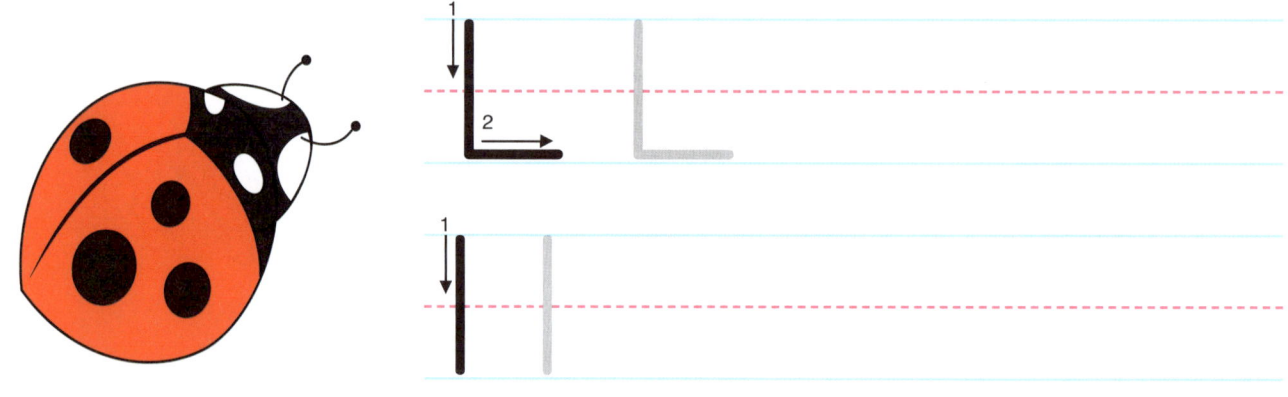

Say the name of each picture. Circle each picture that begins with the /l/ sound, like *ladybug*.

FITNESS FLASH: Do arm circles for 30 seconds.

* See page ii.

Classification/Graphing

DAY 11

Use a red crayon to circle things you can wear. Use a green crayon to circle things you can eat.

1. How many things can you eat? _____

2. How many things can you wear? _____

Neyla saw 5 monkeys, 1 elephant, 4 lions, and 2 bears at the zoo. Color the graph to show the number of each animal that Neyla saw.

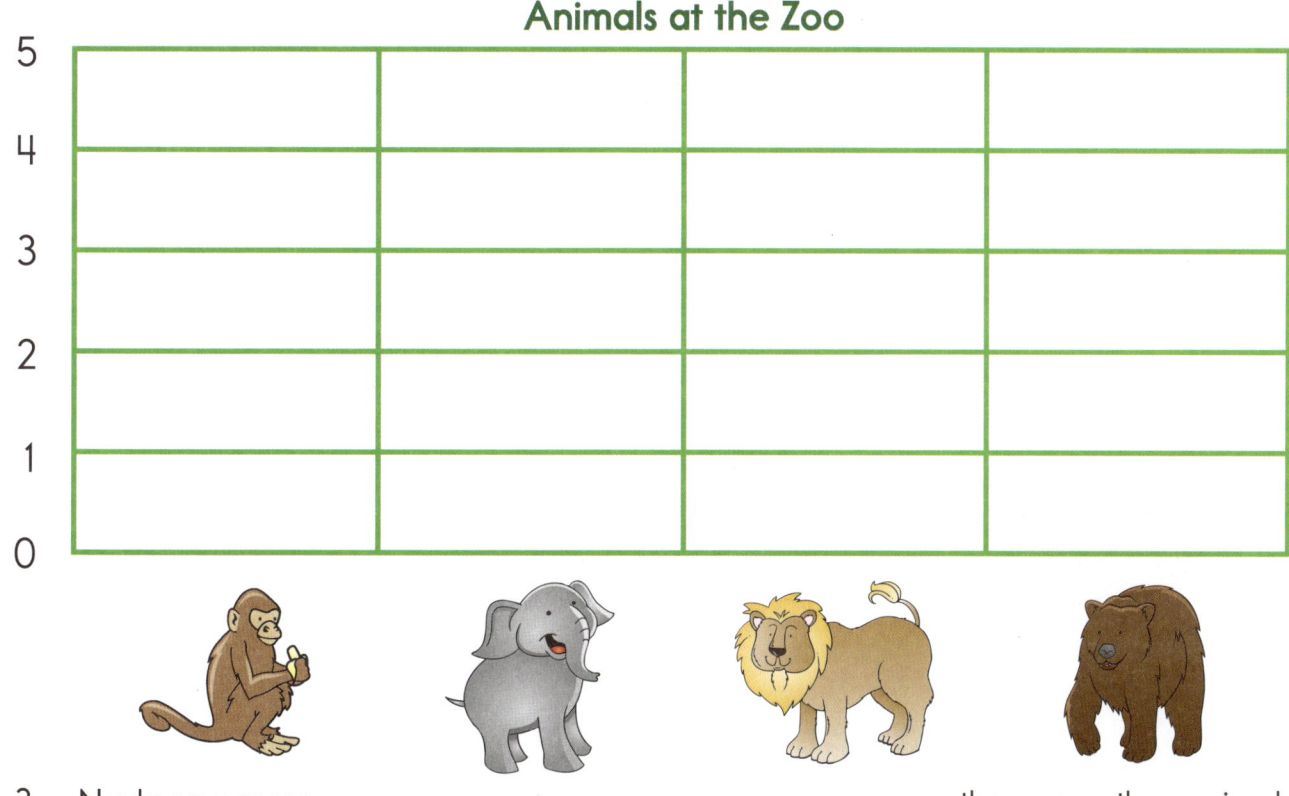

3. Neyla saw more _____ than any other animal.

DAY 11

Handwriting/Phonics

Mouse begins with the /m/ sound. Practice writing uppercase and lowercase **M**s.

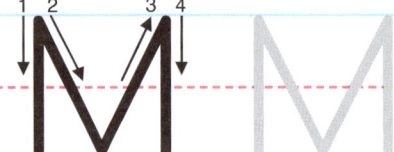
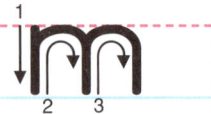

Say the name of each picture. Circle each picture that begins with the /m/ sound, like *mouse*.

CHARACTER CHECK: Think of a time when you did something nice for a friend or family member. How did that make you feel?

Addition & Subtraction

DAY 12

Write a number in each box to solve the addition problem.

10 + 0	10 + 1	10 + 2	10 + 3	10 + 4
10				
10 + 5	10 + 6	10 + 7	10 + 8	10 + 9

Write the missing numbers in each fact family.

1. Family: 4, 6, 10

    4 + ☐ = 10

    4 + 6 = ☐

    10 − ☐ = 6

    10 − 6 = ☐

2. Family: 3, 7, 10

    7 + ☐ = 10

    3 + 7 = ☐

    10 − 3 = ☐

    10 − ☐ = 7

DAY 12

Handwriting/Phonics

Nest begins with the /n/ sound. Practice writing uppercase and lowercase **N**s.

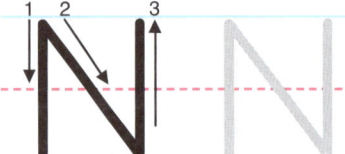

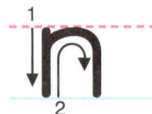

Say the name of each picture. Circle each picture that begins with the /n/ sound, like *nest*.

FACTOID: A hummingbird's nest is about the size of a walnut.

Numbers & Counting/Grammar & Language Arts

DAY 13

Draw a line to match each number to the set with the same number of objects.

1

2

3

4

5

A *noun* is a word that names a person, a place, or a thing. Circle the people. Draw Xs on the places. Draw squares around the things.

girl   school   pencil

farm   baby   desk

DAY 13

Handwriting/Phonics

Parrot begins with the /p/ sound. Practice writing uppercase and lowercase **P**s.

Say the name of each picture. Circle each picture that begins with the /p/ sound, like *parrot*.

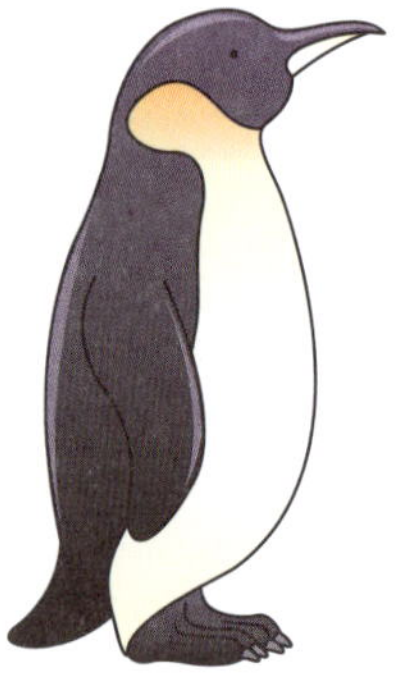

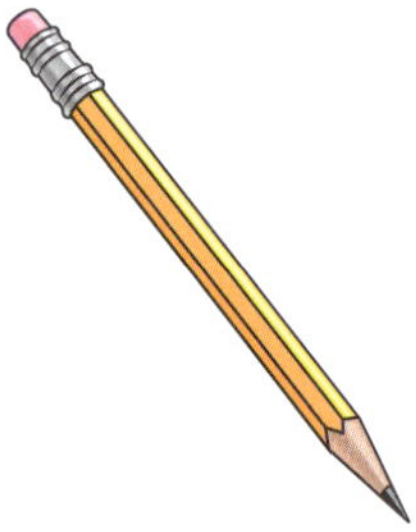

FITNESS FLASH: Do 10 shoulder shrugs.

* See page ii.

Measurement/Phonics

DAY 14

Circle the bowl with more fish.

1.

Circle the plate with fewer cookies.

2.

Say the name of the first picture. Change the first letter to make a new word that names the second picture. Write the new word on the line.

3.

king

4.

sail

5.

cap

CHARACTER CHECK: Write three positive things that you like about yourself.

DAY 14

Handwriting/Phonics

Queen begins with the /kw/ sound. Practice writing uppercase and lowercase **Q**s.

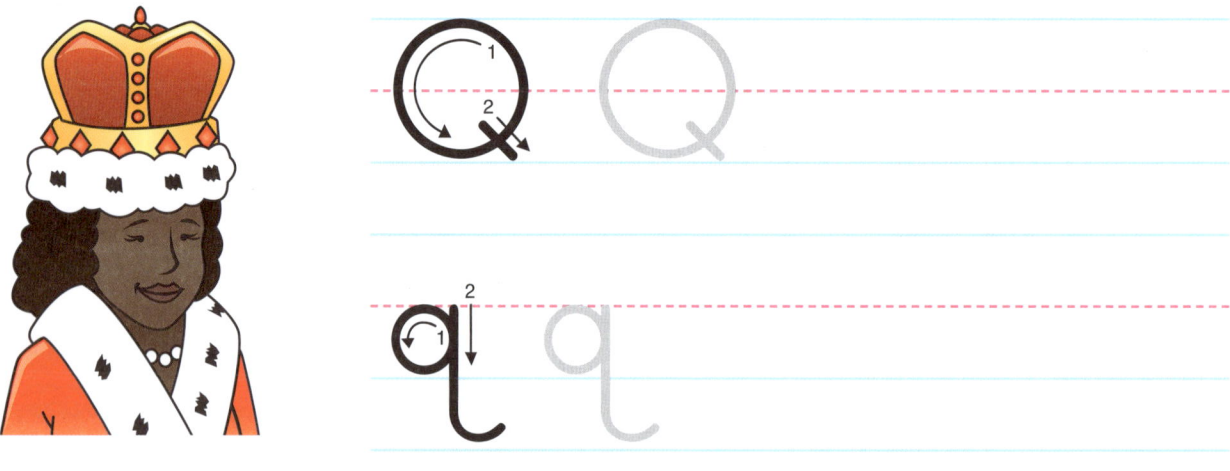

Say the name of each picture. Circle each picture that begins with the /kw/ sound, like *queen*.

FACTOID: The Imperial State Crown of England has more than 3,000 gems.

Numbers & Counting/Fitness

DAY 15

Circle the set with more objects.   Circle the set with fewer objects.

1.

2.

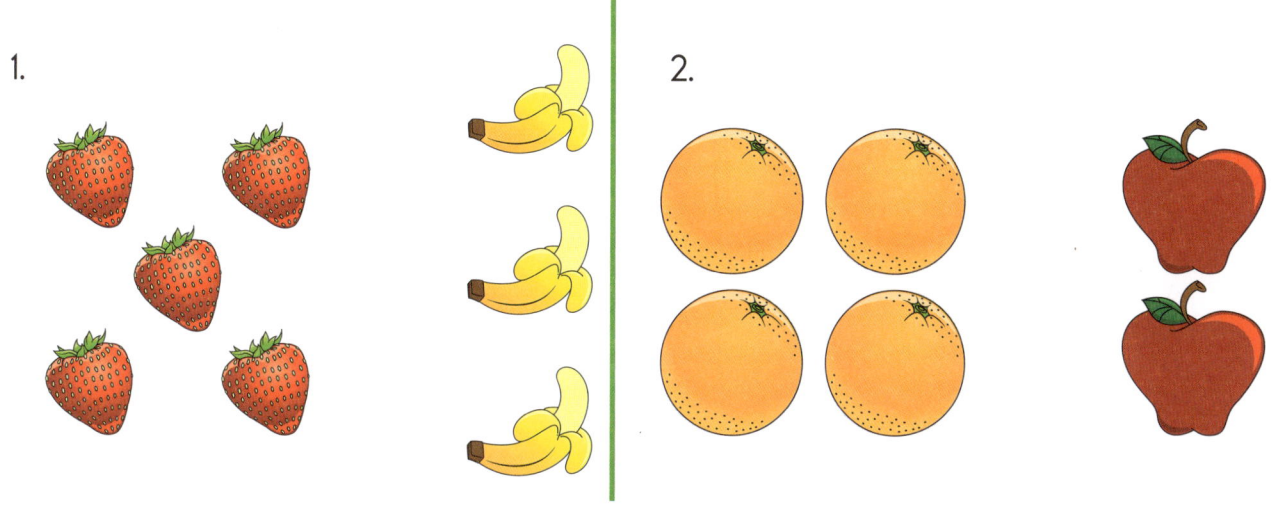

Animal Antics

Stretching exercises will help improve your flexibility. Try the stretch shown on the right. As you stretch, pretend that you are a flexible flamingo. Use your imagination, and you may even forget that you are stretching!

* See page ii.

DAY 15

Handwriting/Phonics

Rug begins with the /r/ sound. Practice writing uppercase and lowercase **R**s.

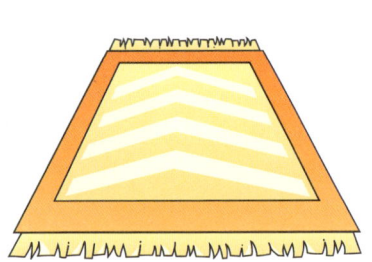
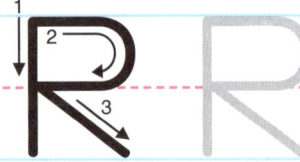
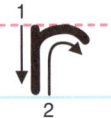

Say the name of each picture. Circle each picture that begins with the /r/ sound, like *rug*.

FITNESS FLASH: Do arm circles for 30 seconds.

* See page ii.

Numbers & Counting/Phonics

DAY 16

Write the missing numbers.

1	2			
			9	
		18		
				25

Draw lines to match the pictures whose names rhyme.

© Carson Dellosa Education

DAY 16

Handwriting/Phonics

Sandwich begins with the /s/ sound. Practice writing uppercase and lowercase **Ss**.

Say the name of each picture. Circle each picture that begins with the /s/ sound, like *sandwich*.

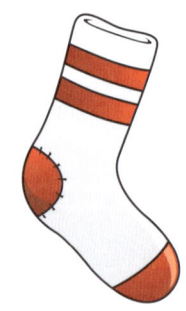

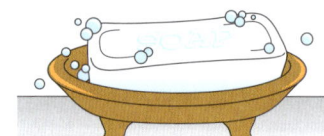

CHARACTER CHECK: Think of two ways that you can be a good friend to someone.

Grammar & Language Arts

DAY 17

Circle the word that names each picture.

1.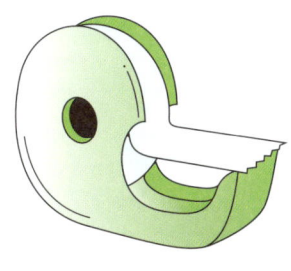

take   tape

2.

mop   map

3.

slid   slide

Write an end mark for each sentence. Choose an end mark from the box.

.   !   ?

4. Do you like cats ☐

5. Ana can swim ☐

6. Can you jump rope ☐

7. That was the best movie ever ☐

8. The girl is new ☐

9. Is Matt in your class ☐

10. Stop doing that ☐

DAY 17

Handwriting/Phonics

Turkey begins with the /t/ sound. Practice writing uppercase and lowercase *T*s.

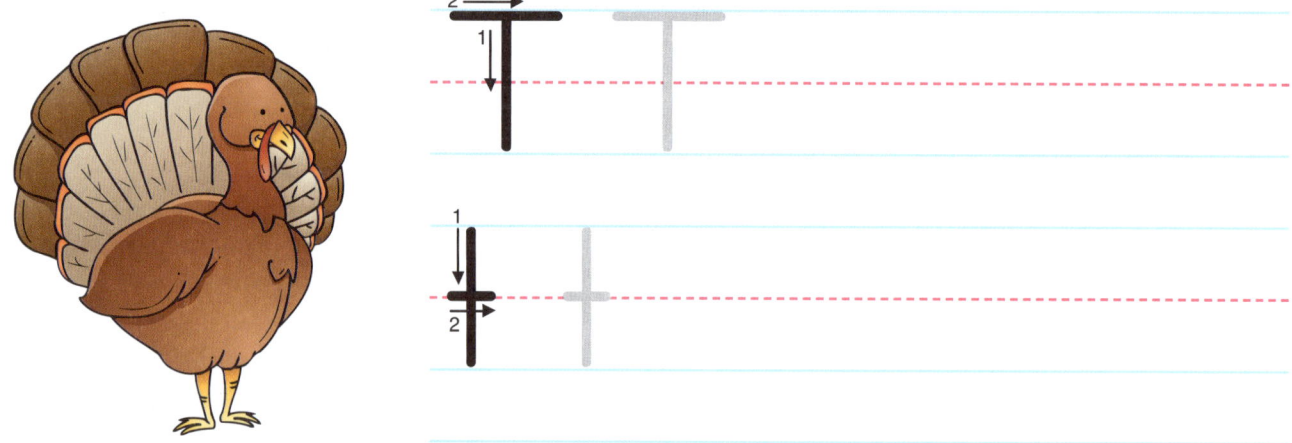

Say the name of each picture. Circle each picture that begins with the /t/ sound, like *turkey*.

FACTOID: An adult turkey can have more than 5,000 feathers.

Grammar & Language Arts

DAY 18

Write the new word on the line.

1. plant + ed = _____
2. dark + er = _____
3. un + happy = _____
4. play + ful = _____
5. re + fill = _____
6. pre + heat = _____

Think of three ways to finish this sentence. Write your sentences on the lines.

I love summer because . . .

7. _____
   _____ .

8. _____
   _____ .

9. _____
   _____ .

DAY 18

Handwriting/Phonics

Vacuum begins with the /v/ sound. Practice writing uppercase and lowercase Vs.

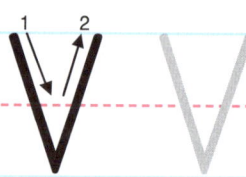

Say the name of each picture. Circle each picture that begins with the /v/ sound, like *vacuum*.

 **FITNESS FLASH:** Touch your toes 10 times.

* See page ii.

Grammar & Language Arts

DAY 19

Add *s* to make each word mean "more than one." Write the new word on the line.

1. bee

2. hat

3. kite

4. sock

Underline the word that completes each sentence.

5. I (see, can) two birds in the tree.

6. Have you seen (it, my) cat?

7. Alex (and, with) Tess are at the library.

8. (The, Come) apple fell on the floor.

9. Ling (are, is) mad at Mom.

10. Dinner is (at, as) 6:00.

DAY 19

Handwriting/Phonics

Wig begins with the /w/ sound. Practice writing uppercase and lowercase Ws.

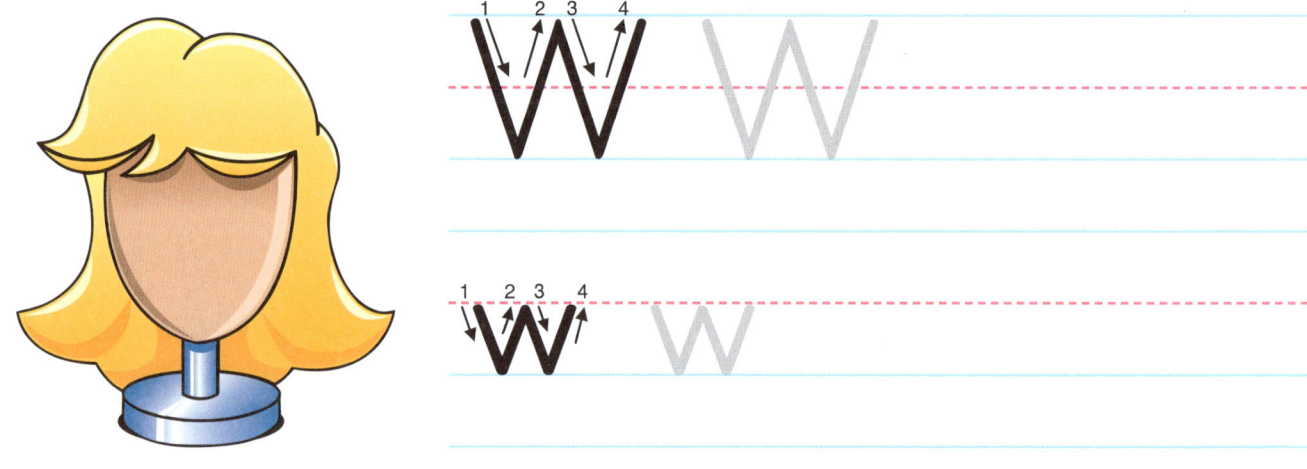

Say the name of each picture. Circle each picture that begins with the /w/ sound, like *wig*.

FACTOID: A walrus's tusks can grow up to three feet (about one meter) long.

Grammar & Language Arts/Character Development

DAY 20

Each question is missing a word. Fill in each blank with a question word from the box.

| Why | Who | What | When | Where |

1. _____ is in the mug?

2. _____ eats ice cream?

3. _____ is the green pail?

4. _____ is Belle on the step?

5. _____ will it rain?

Sharing Success

Show the rewards of sharing. On a separate sheet of paper, draw a picture of a monkey sharing her bananas with two friends. Think about what the monkey and her friends look like as they share the bananas. Are they smiling? Do they look like they are getting along?

DAY 20

Handwriting/Phonics

Fox ends with the /ks/ sound. Practice writing uppercase and lowercase **X**s.

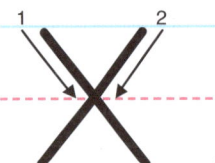
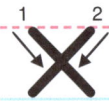

Say the name of each picture. Circle each picture that has the /ks/ sound, like *fox*.

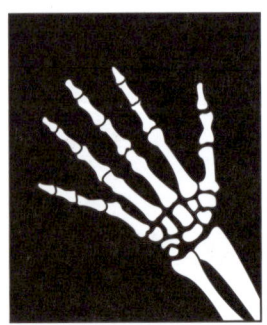
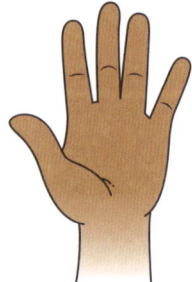

FITNESS FLASH: Practice a V-sit. Stretch three times.

*See page ii.

Science Experiment

BONUS

Wind Direction

Can bubbles be used to find wind direction?

Materials:
- 6 cups (1.4 L) water
- 3/4 cup (180 mL) light corn syrup
- 2 cups (0.5 L) dishwashing liquid
- jar with lid
- large plastic container
- compass
- bubble wand

Procedure:
Have an adult help you measure and pour the water, light corn syrup, and dishwashing liquid into the jar. Cover the jar and shake it. Let the bubbles settle for about four hours.

After the bubble solution has settled, pour it into the large plastic container. Go outside. Have an adult help you use the compass to find north, south, east, and west. Dip the bubble wand into the solution and blow bubbles upward. Watch to see in which direction the wind blows the bubbles.

1. Circle the direction in which the bubbles moved.

   north   south   east   west

2. Circle the direction from which the wind is blowing.

   north   south   east   west

3. What other things outside show from which direction the wind is blowing?

   _____

   _____

BONUS

Science Experiment

Staying Cool

How can you stay cool in the summer?

Materials:
- fan
- sheet of paper towel
- water

Procedure:

Ask an adult to turn on the fan. Move in front of the fan. Then, move away from the fan. Repeat several times to feel the difference. Think about what the air feels like.

Next, wet the paper towel. Place it on your arm. Move in front of the fan. Then, move away from the fan. Repeat several times to feel the difference.

1. Circle which felt cooler.

    A. moving in front of the fan

    B. moving away from the fan

2. Circle which felt cooler.

    A. moving in front of the fan

    B. moving in front of the fan with the wet paper towel on your arm

3. Write two things that would help keep you cool in the summer.

    _____

4. What effect did the fan have on the wet paper towel?

    _____

Social Studies Activity

BONUS

Being a Good Citizen

A good citizen helps the community, protects the environment, follows rules, and treats others with respect. Circle the two pictures that show children being good citizens.

Draw and color a picture that shows how you are a good citizen.

Social Studies Activity

BONUS

Then and Now

Look at the pictures. Circle each picture that shows something made with modern technology.

Social Studies Activity

BONUS

Community Helpers

Look at each picture. Draw a line to match each community helper to the correct tool.

BONUS

Outdoor Extension Activities

Take It Outside!

Look at the picture of a rainbow. Go outside with an adult and try to find one object for each color in the rainbow.

With an adult, find an animal to watch outdoors, such as a frog or squirrel. Do not get too close! Watch how the animal moves. Then, try to move like the animal. Can you do it?

Read the scavenger hunt list. Go outside with an adult. Try to find one object that matches each description.

Scavenger Hunt List

- something wet
- something scratchy
- something soft
- something slimy
- something pretty

- something dry
- something from a tree
- something tall
- something hard
- something blue

*See page ii.

SECTION II

Monthly Goals

Think of three goals that you would like to set for yourself this month. For example, you may want to spend more time reading with your family. Have an adult help you write your goals on the lines.

Place a sticker next to each of your goals that you complete. Feel proud that you have met your goals!

1. _____ [PLACE STICKER HERE]

2. _____ [PLACE STICKER HERE]

3. _____ [PLACE STICKER HERE]

Word List

The following words are used in this section. They are good words for you to know. Read each word aloud with an adult. When you see a word from this list on a page, circle it with your favorite color of crayon.

add	poem
count	puzzles
match	read
opposite	subtract
pattern	touch

SECTION II

Introduction to Strength

This section includes fitness and character development activities that focus on strength. These activities are designed to get your child moving and to get him thinking about strengthening his body and his character. If your child has limited mobility, feel free to modify any suggested exercises to fit individual abilities.

Physical Strength

Like flexibility, strength is an important component of good health. Many children may think that the only people who are strong are people who can lift an enormous amount of weight. However, strength is more than the ability to pick up heavy dumbbells. Explain that strength is built over time and point out to your child how much stronger he has become since he was a toddler.

Everyday activities and many fun exercises provide opportunities for children to gain strength. Your child could carry grocery bags to build his arms, ride a bicycle to develop his legs, or swim for a full-body strength workout. Classic exercises, such as push-ups and chin-ups, are also fantastic strength builders.

Help your child set realistic, achievable goals to improve his strength based on the activities that he enjoys. Over the summer months, offer encouragement and praise as your child gains strength and accomplishes his strength goals.

Strength of Character

As your child is building his physical strength, guide him to work on his inner strength as well. Explain that having strong character means standing up for his values, even if others do not agree with his viewpoint. Explain that it is not always easy to show inner strength. Discuss real-life examples, such as a time that he may have been teased by another child at the playground. How did he use his inner strength to handle the situation?

Remind your child that inner strength can be shown in many ways. For example, your child can show strength by being honest, by standing up for someone who needs his help, and by putting his best efforts into every task. Use your time together over the summer to help your child develop his strength, both physically and emotionally. Look for moments to acknowledge when he has demonstrated strength of character so that he can see the positive growth that he has achieved on the inside.

Addition/Reading Comprehension

DAY 1

Add to find each sum. Place beans on the jar below to help you solve the problems.

1. 1
   +1

2. 2
   +2

3. 1
   +2

4. 3
   +1

5. 2
   +1

6. 3
   +2

7. 1
   +3

8. 2
   +3

Read the story. Answer the questions.

Amad is six. He likes to run. He runs at the park. He runs by the pond. The ducks in the pond watch Amad run. He runs by dogs in the park. The dogs watch him, too. Some kids run with Amad. No one can keep up. Amad is too fast! Amad runs and runs. He is hot, but he does not mind. Then, Amad sees the ice cream truck. Amad will stop running now!

9. Who is a fast runner in the story? _____

10. Where does the story take place? _____

11. Why does Amad stop running at the end? _____

    A. He is tired.

    B. He falls down.

    C. He wants some ice cream.

Handwriting/Phonics

DAY 1

Yo-yo begins with the /y/ sound. Practice writing uppercase and lowercase Ys.

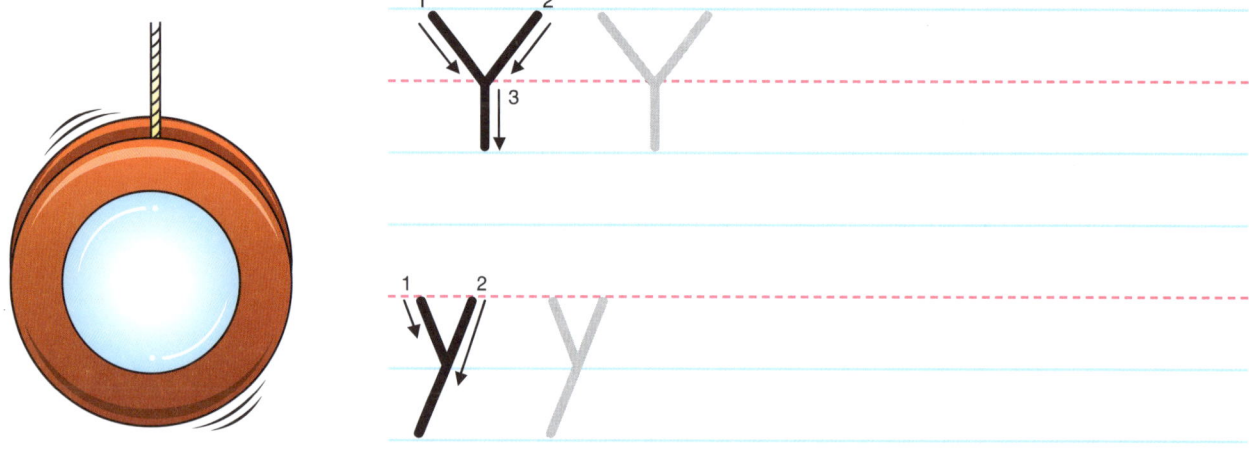

Say the name of each picture. Circle each picture that begins with the /y/ sound, like *yo-yo*.

FACTOID: The oldest yo-yo ever found is about 2,500 years old.

Addition/Fitness

DAY 2

Add to find each sum.

1. 5
   +0

2. 3
   +3

3. 1
   +4

4. 4
   +2

5. 2
   +0

6. 2
   +3

7. 4
   +0

8. 3
   +4

9. 5
   +1

10. 0
    +3

Pull-Up Challenge

Visit a playground with an adult. Ask the adult to show you how to do a pull-up on a jungle gym bar. Try to do one pull-up. Hold on to the jungle gym bar and pull yourself up until your chin goes over the bar. It takes a lot of strength to complete one pull-up!

If you can, try to do more than one pull-up. If you have trouble with this exercise, ask the adult to help you complete a pull-up by holding your lower body as you pull up. Challenge yourself to practice this exercise regularly during the summer to see how many pull-ups you can complete. Have an adult help you set a summer pull-up goal.

* See page ii.

DAY 2

Handwriting/Phonics

Zigzag begins with the /z/ sound. Practice writing uppercase and lowercase Zs.

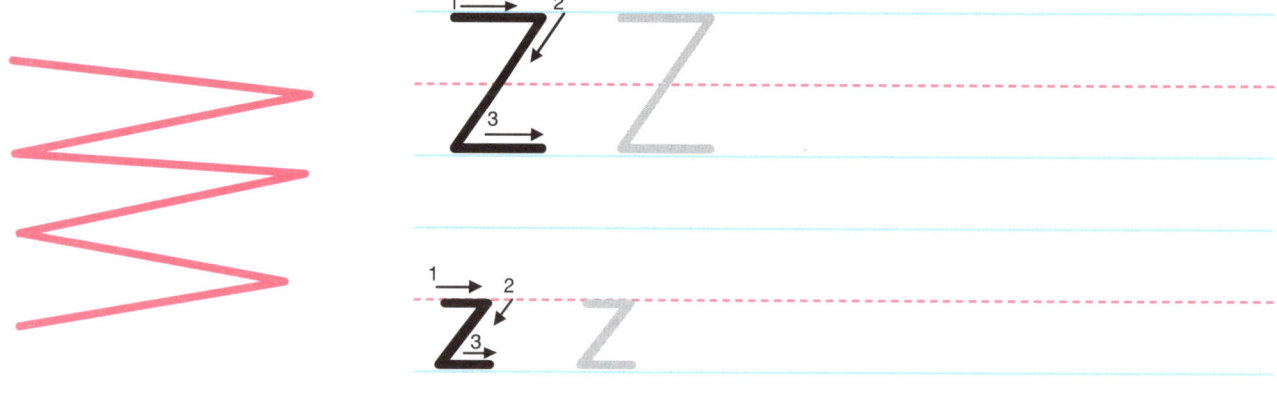

Say the name of each picture. Circle each picture that begins with the /z/ sound, like *zigzag*.

FITNESS FLASH: Do 10 lunges.

* See page ii.

Addition/Graphing

DAY 3

Add to find each sum.

1. 3 + 1 = _____
2. 4 + 1 = _____
3. 3 + 0 = _____

4. 2 + 2 = _____
5. 1 + 3 = _____
6. 5 + 0 = _____

Count the animals on the farm. Color one box for each animal you count.

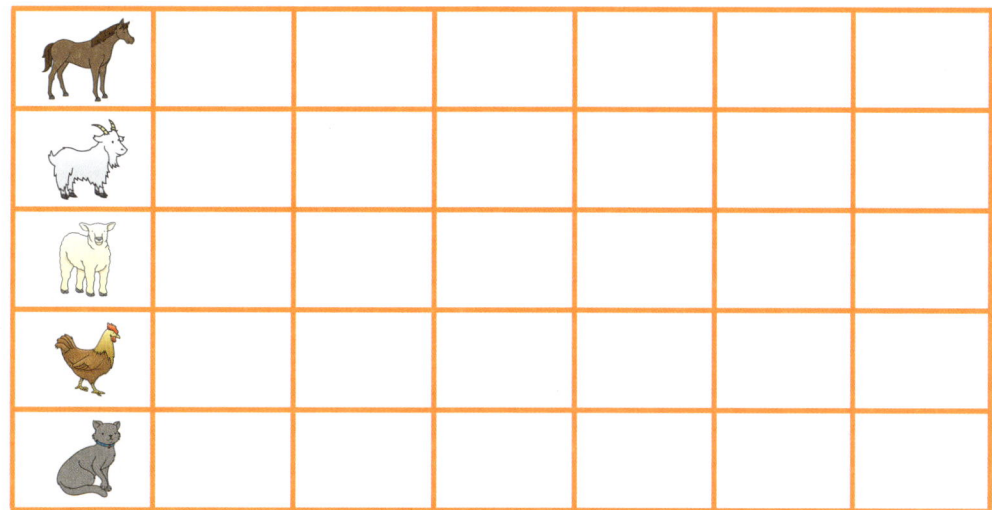

7. Are there more sheep or cats? _____

8. How many roosters are there? _____

DAY 3

Handwriting/Phonics

Ant begins with the short *a* sound. Practice writing uppercase and lowercase **A**s.

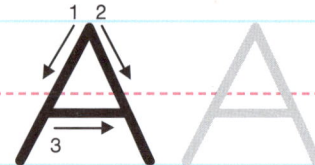

Say the name of each picture. Circle each picture that has the short *a* sound, like *ant*.

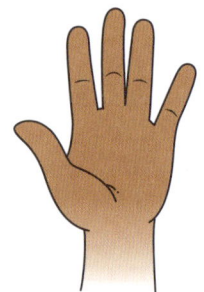

FACTOID: An ant can lift 10-50 times its own weight.

Measurement/Numbers & Counting

DAY 4

Follow the directions.

1. Draw an X on the largest plate.

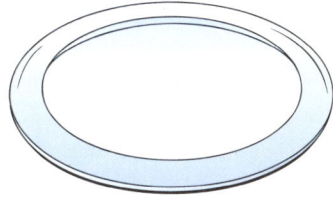 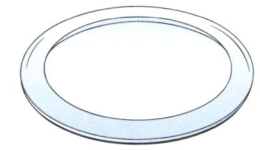 

2. Circle the smallest spoon.

 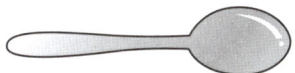 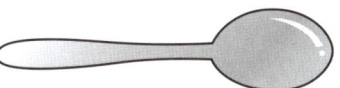

3. Circle the largest pie. Draw an X on the smallest pie.

Write the missing numbers.

DAY 4

Phonics

Say the name of each picture. Write the missing short *a*.
EXAMPLE:

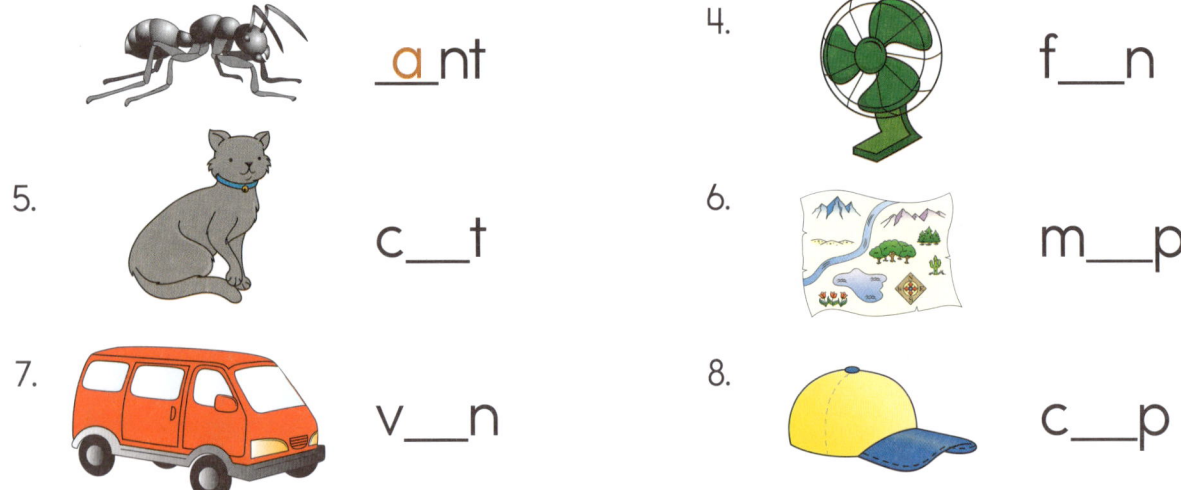

_a_nt

4. f__n

5. c__t

6. m__p

7. v__n

8. c__p

Say each word. Listen for the short *a* sound. Draw an X on the word that does not have the short *a* sound.

man

ant

ran

sad

bed

bag

can

had

tag

FITNESS FLASH: Do five push-ups.

* See page ii.

Numbers & Counting/Character Development

DAY 5

Follow the directions.

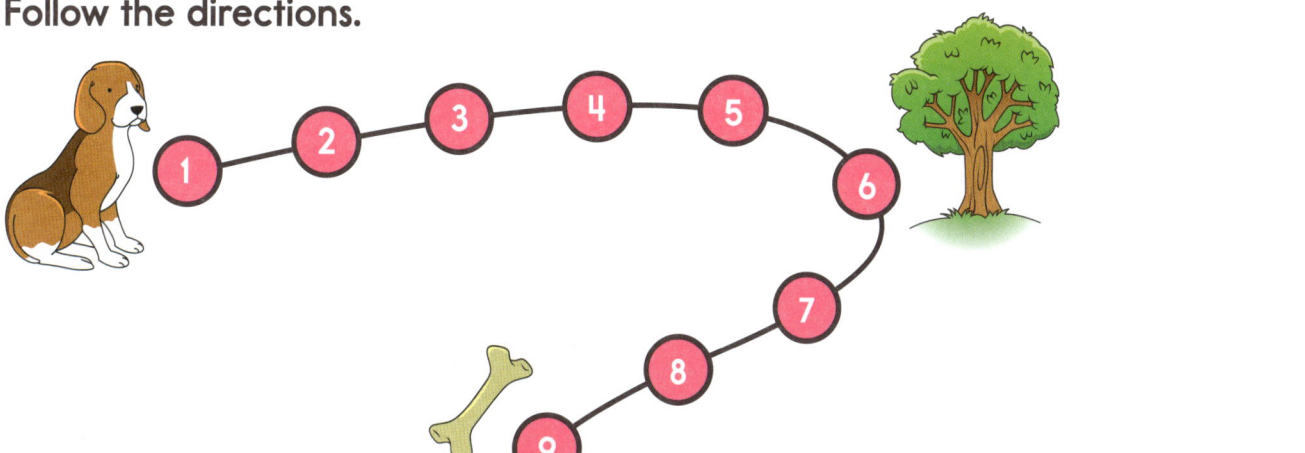

1. Fido takes 6 steps forward. What is he standing beside? _____

2. Then, Fido takes 1 step backward. He takes 4 steps forward. What does Fido find?
   _____

3. How many more steps must Fido take until he reaches his doghouse?
   _____

Honesty Journal

Being honest means being truthful. Make an honesty journal with an adult. Fold a sheet of construction paper to make the cover. Place blank paper inside the cover. Staple along the left side. Write the title, *A True Look at Honesty*, on the front cover. Use craft supplies to decorate the cover.

Draw pictures of yourself acting honestly. Show and explain what happens when you tell the truth and what happens when you do not tell the truth. Show your honesty journal to an adult. Talk about your drawings.

DAY 5

Phonics/Reading Comprehension

Read the poem aloud. Listen for the short *a* sound. Draw a line under each word that has the short *a* sound.

Sam and Max

Sam has a cat.
Sam's cat is Max.
Max is a good cat.

Sam has a cap.
Max likes the cap.
Max sits on Sam's lap.

Sam has a bag.
Max runs to the bag.
Max naps on Sam's bag.

Read the poem again. Then, answer the questions.

4. Which sentence tells what the poem is about?
    A. Sam has a cat.
    B. Max likes to wear a cap.
    C. Max is a sleepy cat.

5. Where did Max nap?
    A. on the bed
    B. on Sam's bag
    C. on a mat

6. How do you think Max feels when he sits on Sam's lap?
    A. happy
    B. sad
    C. scared

FACTOID: The longest whiskers ever measured on a cat were 7.5 inches (19 cm) long.

© Carson Dellosa Education

Subtraction/Grammar & Language Arts

DAY 6

Subtract to find each difference. Place beans on the jar below to help you solve the problems.

1. 2 − 1
2. 3 − 2
3. 4 − 1
4. 5 − 2

5. 3 − 1
6. 2 − 2
7. 4 − 3
8. 5 − 3

Common nouns name people, places, and things. *Proper nouns* name specific people, places, and things. Read each pair. Write *C* next to the common nouns. Write *P* next to the proper nouns.

9. ____ girl

    ____ Anna

10. ____ Park Street Elementary

    ____ school

11. ____ Mr. Jones

    ____ man

12. ____ city

    ____ Boston

CHARACTER CHECK: Write five things that you are thankful for. Share your list with an adult.

DAY 6

Handwriting/Phonics

Egg begins with the short *e* sound. Practice writing uppercase and lowercase *E*s.

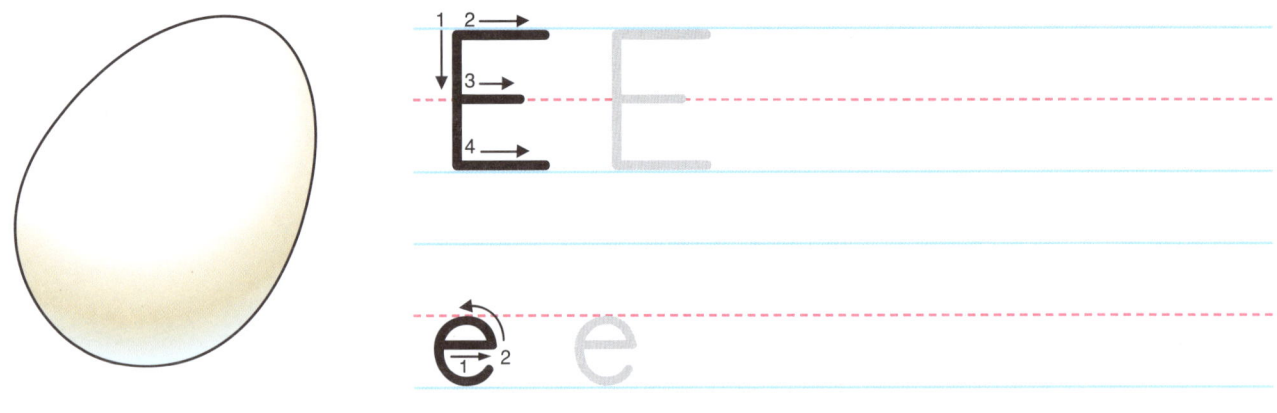

Say the name of each picture. Circle each picture that has the short *e* sound, like *egg*.

DAY 7

Subtraction/Grammar & Language Arts

Subtract to find each difference.

1. 5
   −1

2. 6
   −2

3. 6
   −3

4. 5
   −5

5. 5
   −4

6. 4
   −2

7. 2
   −1

8. 3
   −3

9. 6
   −1

10. 3
    −0

Write *S* on the line next to sentences. Draw an X next to words that are not sentences.

11. _____ by the cat

12. _____ My dad grew up on a farm.

13. _____ all the way to the store

14. _____ Dante has that book, too.

15. _____ It might rain today.

DAY 7

Phonics

Say the name of each picture. Write the missing short *e*.

EXAMPLE:

b_e_ll

16. t__nt

17. p__n

18. v__st

19. __gg

20. n__st

Say each word. Listen for the short *e* sound. Draw an X on the word that does not have the short *e* sound.

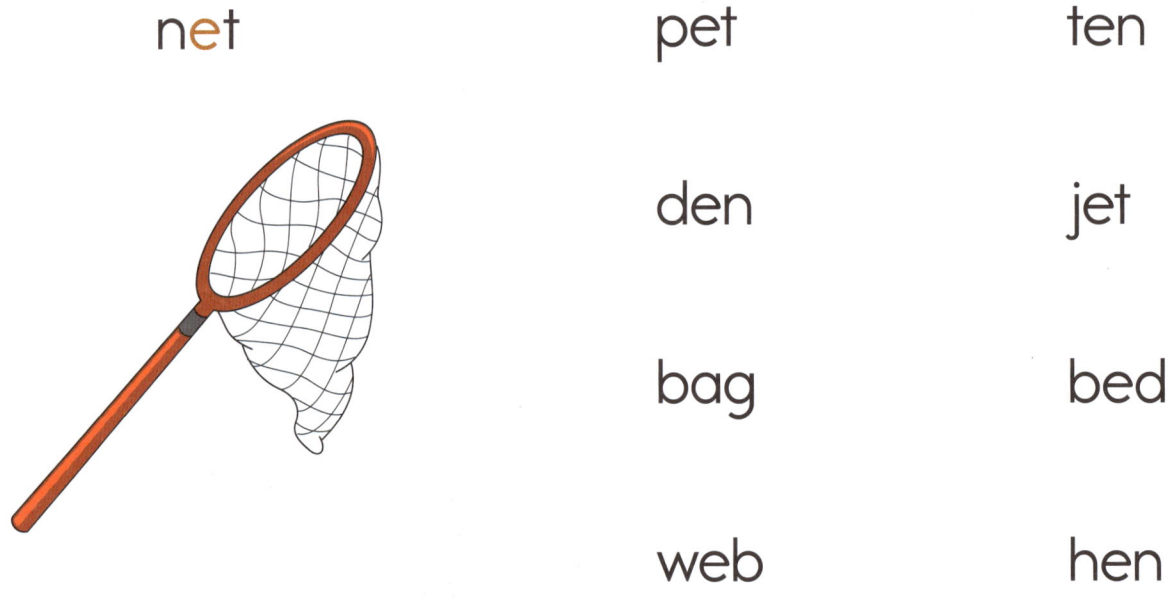

n**e**t

pet   ten

den   jet

bag   bed

web   hen

FACTOID: Lions live in groups called *prides*.

Subtraction/Time

DAY 8

Subtract to find each difference.

1. 3 – 1 = _____
2. 3 – 2 = _____
3. 4 – 2 = _____

4. 4 – 1 = _____
5. 5 – 4 = _____
6. 5 – 3 = _____

Look at each clock. Write the time shown.

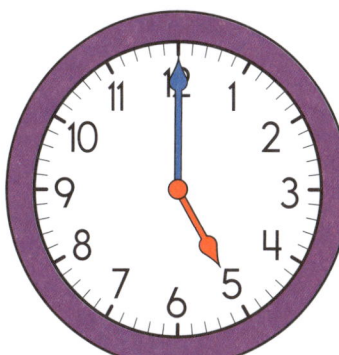

___ : ___   ___ : ___   ___ : ___

___ : ___   ___ : ___   ___ : ___

FITNESS FLASH: Do 10 squats.

* See page ii.

DAY 8

Phonics/Reading Comprehension

Read the poem aloud. Listen for the short *e* sound. Draw a line under each word that has the short *e* sound.

Meg the Vet

Meg is a vet.
Vets help sick pets.
Vets help pets get well.
Some vets help big pets.
Some vets help small pets.

Vets can wrap a dog's leg.
Vets can mend a horse's head.
Vets can fix a cat with no pep.
Vets can also help your pet.
Meg likes being a vet.

Read the poem again. Then, answer the questions.

7. Which sentence tells what the poem is about?

    A. Pets get sick.

    B. Vets help sick pets.

    C. Cats have no pep.

8. Whom do vets help? _____

9. Write *T* for things that are true. Write *F* for things that are false.

    _____ Meg likes being a vet.

    _____ Vets help small pets.

    _____ Vets fix cars.

CHARACTER CHECK: Write a song about respecting all of Earth's creatures. Share your song with an adult.

66

© Carson Dellosa Education

PLACE STICKER HERE

Subtraction/Measurement

DAY 9

Subtract to find each difference.

1. 7
   −3

2. 6
   −5

3. 9
   −4

4. 6
   −4

5. 9
   −8

6. 8
   −8

7. 8
   −5

8. 5
   −5

9. 6
   −2

10. 7
    −6

Circle the boy who is taller.

Circle the cup that is more full.

Circle the cat that is darker.

Circle the ball that is smaller.

DAY 9

Handwriting/ Phonics

Iguana begins with the short *i* sound. Practice writing uppercase and lowercase **I**s.

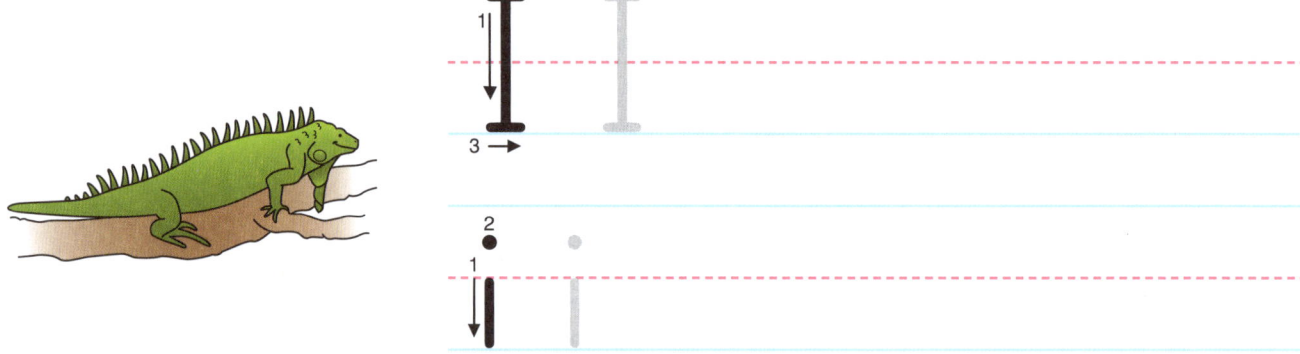

Say the name of each picture. Circle each picture that has the short *i* sound, like *iguana*.

FACTOID: Safety pins have been used for more than 2,500 years.

Visual Discrimination/Addition & Subtraction

DAY 10

Circle the numbers that match the first number in each row.

12	21	12	15	12	51	12	21	12
96	96	99	66	86	96	66	96	96
54	55	54	45	43	54	45	54	52
71	71	17	71	11	71	71	17	71
35	53	55	35	35	33	35	53	35

Look at each number in the leaf. On the leaf to the left, write the number that is 10 less. On the leaf to the right, write the number that is 10 more.

1. 30
2. 85
3. 42
4. 70

DAY 10

Phonics

Say the name of each picture. Write the missing short *i*.

EXAMPLE:

   w_i_g

5.    s___nk

6.    m___lk

7.    b___b

8.    sh___p

9.    s___x

Say each word. Listen for the short *i* sound. Draw an X on the word that does not have the short *i* sound.

pin

did   hid

bug   win

in   it

sit   is

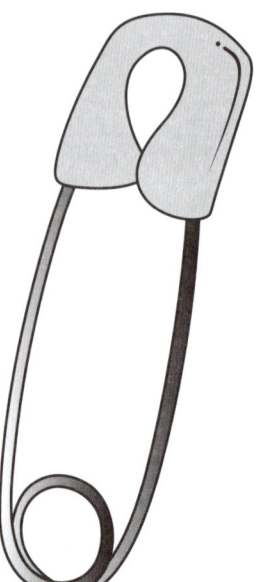

 **FITNESS FLASH:** Do 10 lunges.

* See page ii.

Numbers & Counting/Shape Recognition

DAY 11

Count the tens. Write each number.

1.  _____
2. 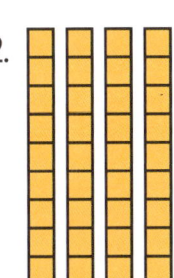 _____
3. 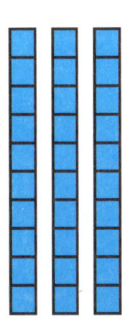 _____
4. 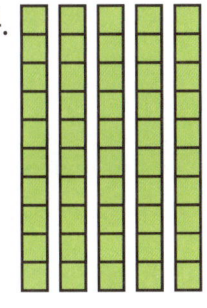 _____
5. 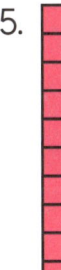 _____
6. 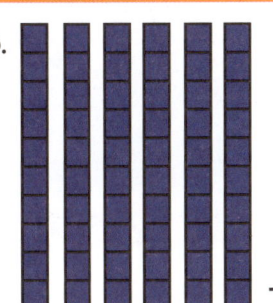 _____

Draw a shape to match each item below.

EXAMPLE:

 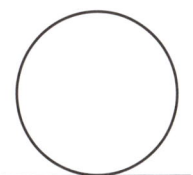    _____

 _____    _____

 _____    _____

DAY 11

Handwriting/Phonics

Ostrich begins with the short *o* sound. Practice writing uppercase and lowercase Os.

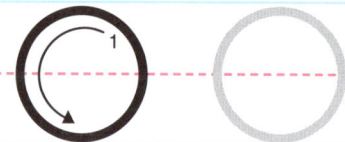

Say the name of each picture. Circle each picture that has the short *o* sound, like *ostrich*.

  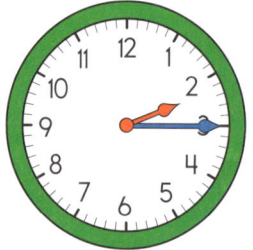

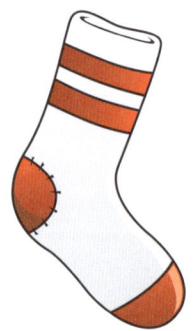  

FITNESS FLASH: Do five push-ups.

* See page ii.

Addition & Subtraction/Measurement

DAY 12

Complete each fact family.

1. Family: 3, 5, 8

   5 + 3 = ☐

   ☐ + ☐ = 8

   8 − ☐ = ☐

   ☐ − 3 = ☐

2. Family: 2, 8, 10

   8 + 2 = ☐

   ☐ + 8 = 10

   10 − ☐ = 2

   10 − ☐ = 8

3. Family: 2, 3, 5

   2 + 3 = ☐

   3 + ☐ = 5

   5 − 2 = ☐

   ☐ − 3 = 2

Draw a line under the shortest thing. Circle the longest thing.

DAY 12

Phonics

Say the name of each object. Write the missing short o.
EXAMPLE:

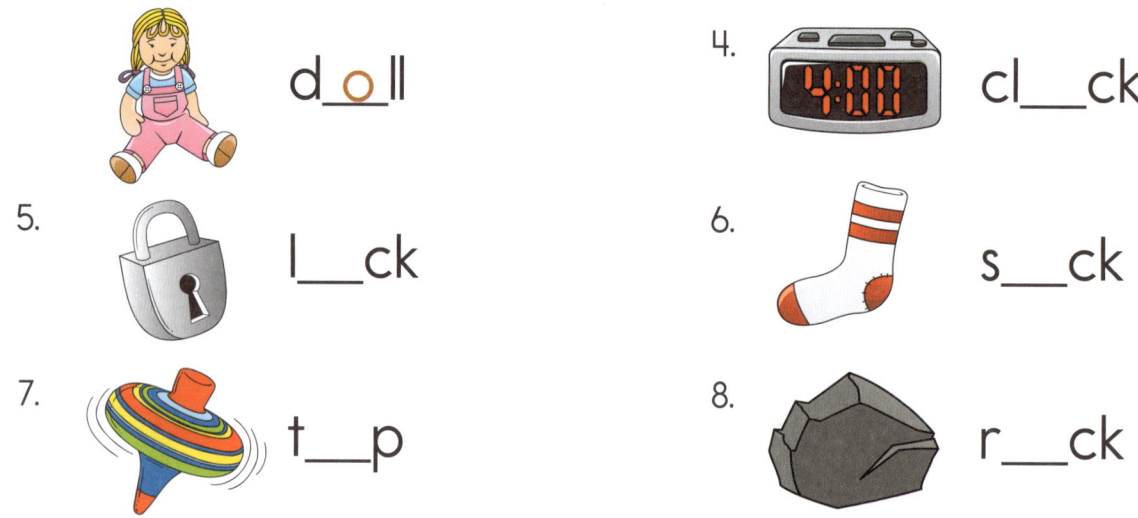

d_o_ll

4. cl__ck

5. l__ck

6. s__ck

7. t__p

8. r__ck

Say each word. Listen for the short o sound. Draw an X on the word that does not have the short o sound.

fox

dog   top

hot   fog

box   got

pop   bib

CHARACTER CHECK: What does it mean to be brave? Look up the word in a dictionary with an adult.

Measurement/Addition & Subtraction

DAY 13

Circle the largest object in each group.

Circle the smallest object in each group.

Read each equation. If it is true, circle it. If it is false, draw an X on it.

5. 3 + 11 = 13

6. 15 + 5 = 20

7. 10 − 7 = 3

8. 9 + 4 = 14

9. 12 − 8 = 20

10. 13 − 13 = 0

11. 7 + 8 = 16

12. 4 + 4 = 8

13. 19 − 6 = 13

14. 15 − 5 = 11

DAY 13

Phonics/Reading Comprehension

Read the poem aloud. Listen for the short *o* sound. Draw a line under each word that has the short *o* sound.

Rob the Dog

A frog sat on a log by the pond.
Along came a dog named Rob.
Rob, the dog, sat on the log.
The dog sang a song.
The frog did not like the song.
The frog hopped off the log.

Along came a fox.
The fox sat on the log.
Rob, the dog, sat on the log.
The dog sang a song.
The fox did not like the song.
The fox popped off the log.

Read the poem again. Then, answer the questions.

15. Which animal sang the song? _____

16. Why did the frog leave the log?

    A. The fox sat on the log.   B. The dog sat on the log.

    C. The frog did not like the song.   D. The frog wanted to sing.

17. How did the frog leave the log? _____

18. How did the fox leave the log? _____

19. Write another good title for the poem. _____

FITNESS FLASH: Do 10 squats.

* See page ii.

Addition & Subtraction/Numbers & Counting

DAY 14

Solve the word problems.

1. Riley spent 8¢ on stickers. Tasha spent 10¢. How much did they spend altogether?

   _____

2. Suki has 4 stamps. Owen has 11 stamps. How many stamps do they have altogether?

   _____

3. Rico has 12 comic books. He lent Patrick 4. How many comic books does Rico have now?

   _____

4. Emma has 19 balloons. Luna popped 8. How many balloons does Emma have now?

   _____

Draw a line to match each number to the set with the same number of objects.

16

18

20

DAY 14

Handwriting/Phonics

Umbrella begins with the short *u* sound. Practice writing uppercase and lowercase Us.

Say the name of each picture. Circle each picture that has the short *u* sound, like *umbrella*.

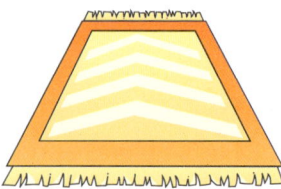  

FACTOID: *Parasol* is another word for *umbrella*.

Grammar & Language Arts

DAY 15

Look at the picture. Read each question. Circle the correct answer.

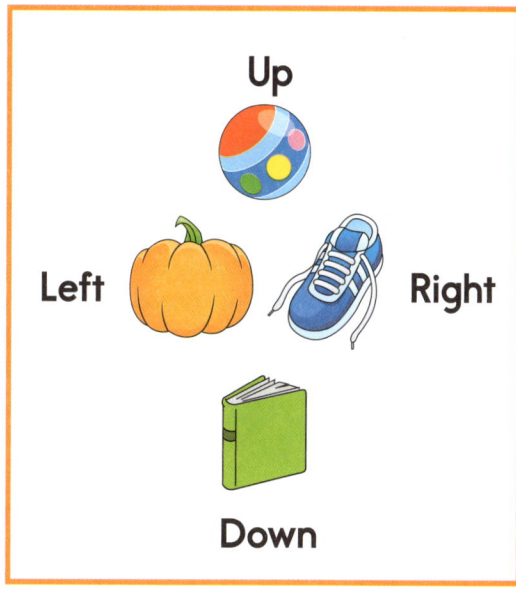

1. What is up?
2. What is down?
3. What is left?
4. What is right?

Write the name of each picture to solve the crossword puzzles.

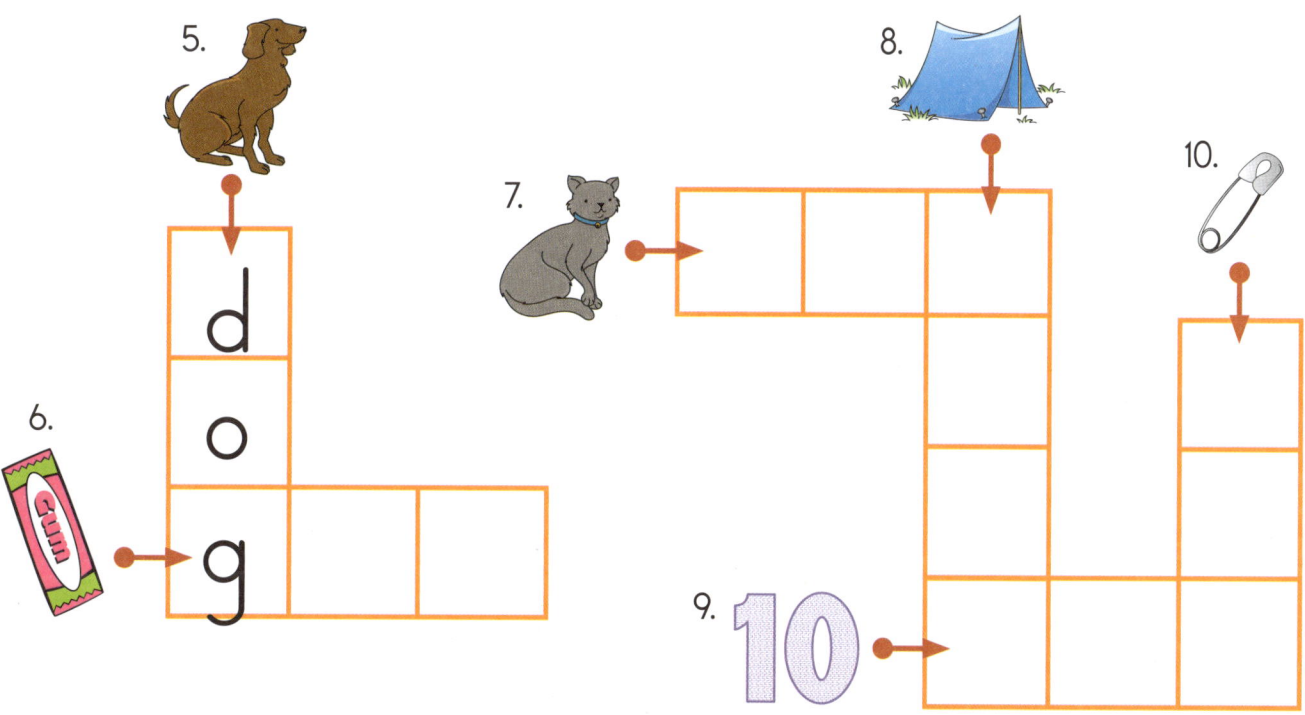

DAY 15

Phonics

Say the name of each picture. Write the missing short *u*.

EXAMPLE:

h_u_g

12. d___ck

14. t___b

11.  r___g

13. s___n

15. m___g

Say each word. Listen for the short *u* sound. Draw an X on the word that does not have the short *u* sound.

gum

mud

dug

cut

up

fun

hat

us

hut

FITNESS FLASH: Do 10 sit-ups.

* See page ii.

Measurement/Grammar & Language Arts

DAY 16

Circle the object in each group that holds more.

1.

2.

Circle the object in each group that holds less.

3.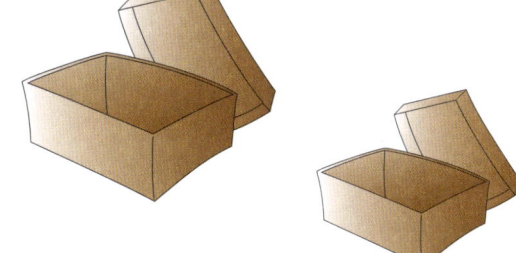

4.

Draw a line to match each opposite.

up

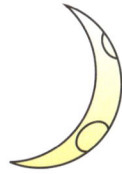

night

happy

day

sad

down

Grammar & Language Arts/Phonics

DAY 16

A *pronoun* takes the place of a noun. Fill in each blank with a pronoun from the box.

| I | her | him | it | We | they |

5. Will gave the gift to _____ after school.

6. Who put _____ on the table?

7. _____ will meet you at the park.

8. Lita and Erik are best friends, but _____ live far apart.

9. Nick passed the ball to _____.

10. _____ feed the birds in our yard.

Circle the letters that make the sound you hear at the start of each word.

11.
sh   th   ch

12.
th   ch   sh

13.
ch   sh   wh

14.
wh   th   sh

15.
ch   th   sh

Phonics/Fitness

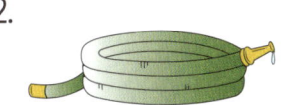

DAY 17

Read each word. If it has a long vowel sound, write *L* on the line. If it has a short vowel sound, write *S*.

1.    sock
   _____

2.    hose
   _____

3.    sun
   _____

4. 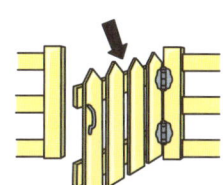   chick
   _____

5.    grapes
   _____

6.    gate
   _____

7. five
   _____

8. bell
   _____

Arm Curls

Collect empty water bottles of different sizes. Hold an empty water bottle in each hand and do arm curls. Fill the bottles with water. Make sure that the lids are on tight! Try to do arm curls with the full bottles. Which bottles take more strength to lift, the larger or smaller bottles? How many arm curls can you do with each arm?

* See page ii.

DAY 17

Phonics/Grammar & Language Arts

Circle the vowel sound you hear in each syllable.

9.

sev   en

e i   u e

10.

win   dow

a i   u o

11.

fish

e i

12.

bee

a e

13.

rab   bit

i a   i u

Everyone gets scared sometimes. Tell about a time you felt scared. What made you feel better? Use complete sentences. Ask an adult if you need help.

_____

_____

_____

_____

Reading Comprehension

DAY 18

Read the passage. Answer the questions.

Pups and Cubs

Pups and cubs are little and cute. Pups make good pets. Cubs do not.

Pups are baby dogs. They like to run. Cubs are baby bears. They like to run, too. You can run with pups but not with cubs. A pup's mother would be glad if you ran with her pup. But, a cub's mother would be mad if you ran with her cub.

Pups and cubs like to tug. Pups are fun to play tug with, but a cub's tug can be too much! So, pick a pup for a pet, not a cub.

1. Which sentence tells what the passage is about?

    A. Cubs like to run.

    B. Pups make good pets, but cubs do not.

    C. Pups and cubs are cute.

2. What is a pup?

    A. a mother bear

    B. a baby bear

    C. a baby dog

3. Is this passage fiction or nonfiction?

FACTOID: There are eight species of bears in the world.

DAY 18

Phonics/Shape Recognition

Say the name of each picture. Draw a line to match each picture to the letters that spell the long vowel sound.

   a___e

   oa

   ee

   i___e

Write how many sides and corners each shape has.

	Sides	Corners		Sides	Corners
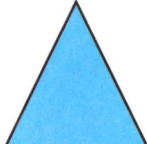	___	___		___	___
	___	___		___	___
	___	___		___	___

Numbers & Counting

DAY 19

Touch each number in order. Say it aloud with an adult. Use the red numbers to count by tens.

1	2	3	4	5	6	7	8	9	10
11	12	13	14	15	16	17	18	19	20
21	22	23	24	25	26	27	28	29	30
31	32	33	34	35	36	37	38	39	40
41	42	43	44	45	46	47	48	49	50
51	52	53	54	55	56	57	58	59	60
61	62	63	64	65	66	67	68	69	70
71	72	73	74	75	76	77	78	79	80
81	82	83	84	85	86	87	88	89	90
91	92	93	94	95	96	97	98	99	100
101	102	103	104	105	106	107	108	109	110
111	112	113	114	115	116	117	118	119	120

© Carson Dellosa Education

DAY 19

Grammar & Language Arts

Underline the verb that completes each sentence.

1. Hal (swim, swims) in the fish bowl.

2. The girls (jump, jumps) into the pool.

3. The red leaf (fall, falls) to the ground.

4. The cups (is, are) on the table.

Read each pair of sentences. Make a check mark ✔ next to the one that is not missing any capital letters.

5. _____ carlos and ben will meet us soon.

   _____ Carlos and Ben will meet us soon.

6. _____ Mr. Chen lives on my block.

   _____ Mr. chen lives on my block.

7. _____ Kate, lena, and yoshi ate all the peaches.

   _____ Kate, Lena, and Yoshi ate all the peaches.

8. _____ I think Zack can cross the monkey bars.

   _____ i think zack can cross the monkey bars.

Numbers & Counting/Time

DAY 20

On each number line, draw a dot on the first number. Then, skip-count by twos. Draw a dot on each number in the pattern. The first pattern has been started for you.

1.
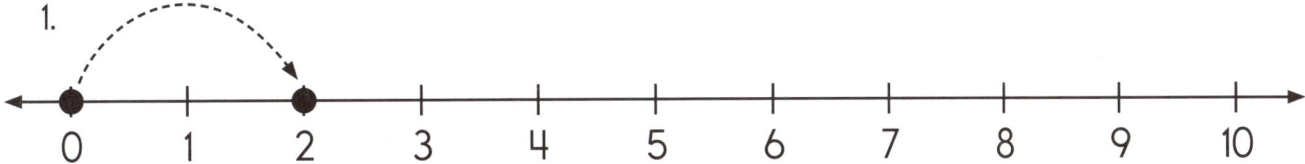

2.
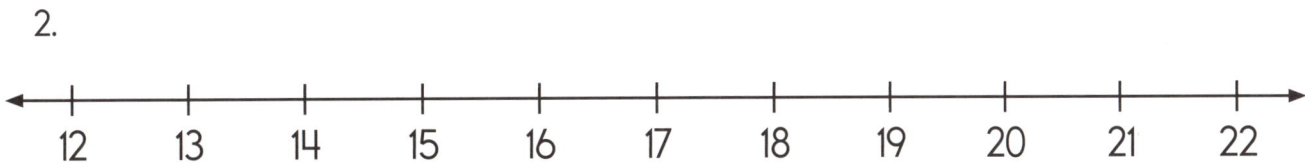

Use the calendar to answer each question.

July

Sunday	Monday	Tuesday	Wednesday	Thursday	Friday	Saturday
		1	2	3	4	5
6	7	8	9	10	11	12
13	14	15	16	17	18	19
20	21	22	23	24	25	26
27	28	29	30	31		

3. What day of the week is July 23? _____

4. What day of the week is the last day of July? _____

5. What date is the second Tuesday? _____

6. What day of the week is July 4? _____

DAY 20

Classification/Grammar & Language Arts

Read each word. What category does it belong in? Write the number of the category on the line.

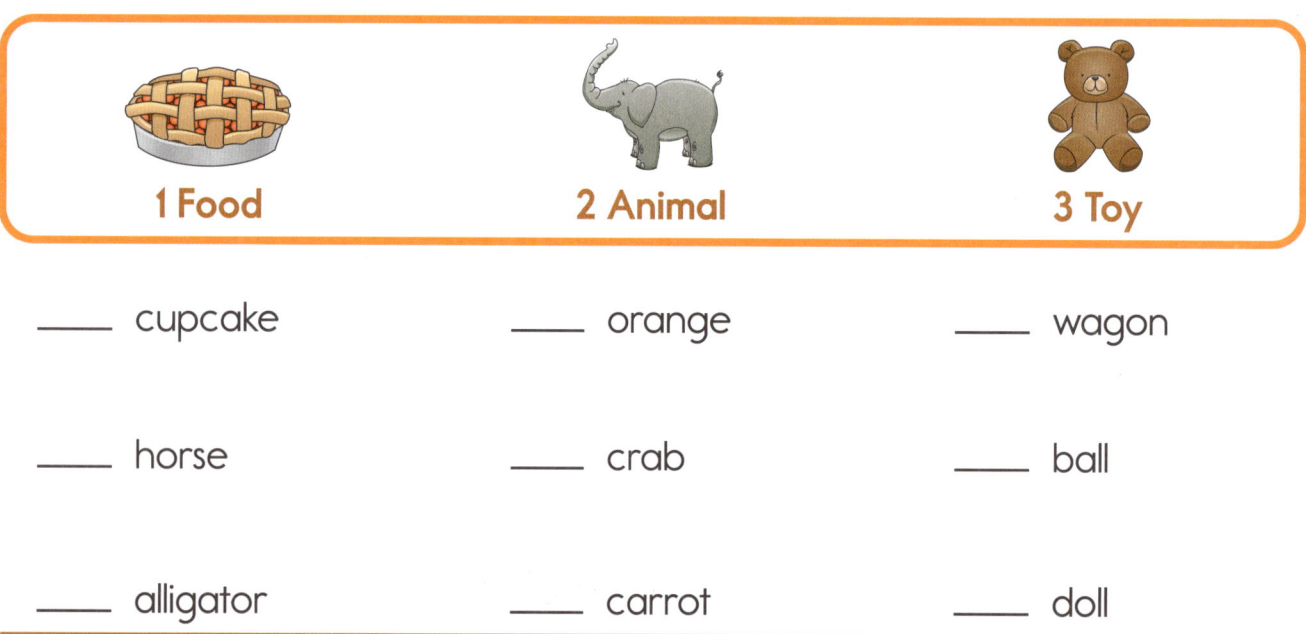

1 Food   2 Animal   3 Toy

____ cupcake   ____ orange   ____ wagon

____ horse   ____ crab   ____ ball

____ alligator   ____ carrot   ____ doll

For each word, take away the underlined letters. Write the root word on the line.

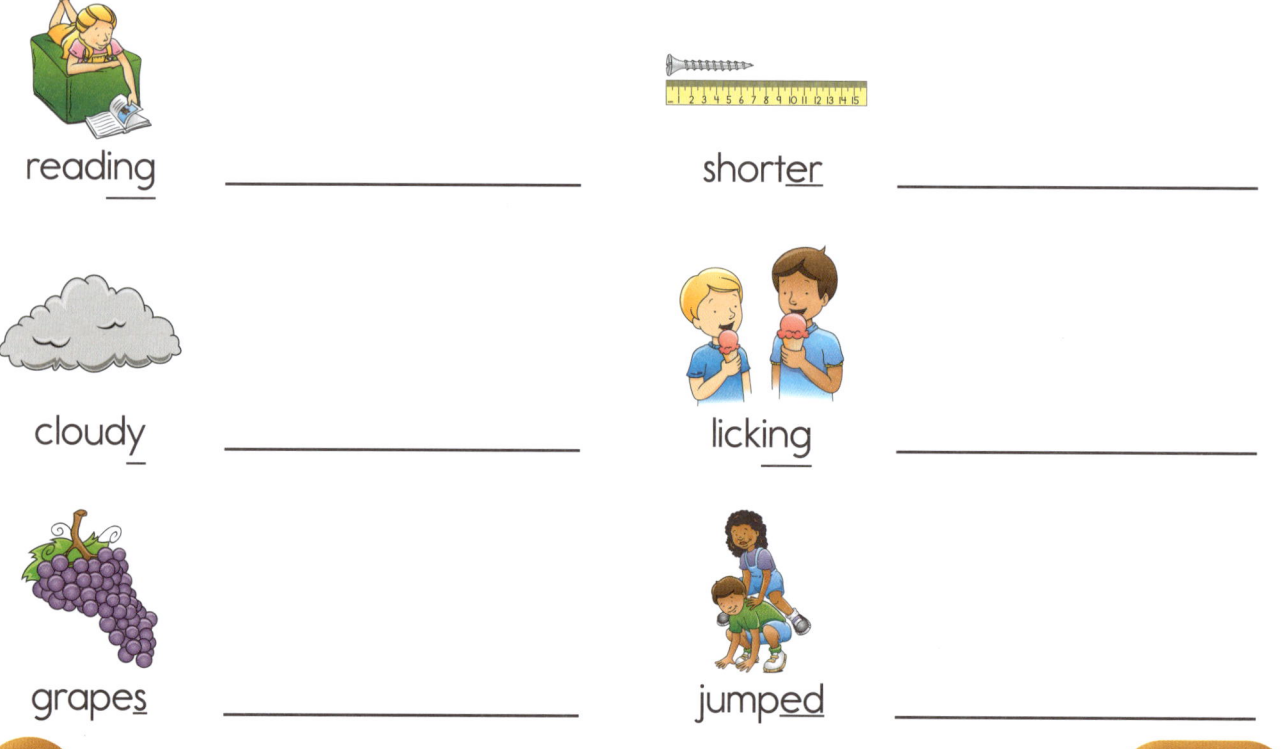

read<u>ing</u>   _____   shor<u>ter</u>   _____

cloud<u>y</u>   _____   lick<u>ing</u>   _____

grape<u>s</u>   _____   jump<u>ed</u>   _____

Science Experiment

Constellations

A *constellation* is a group of stars that make a pattern. How can you make a constellation in your room?

Materials:
- flashlight
- round cardboard container
- sharpened pencil

Procedure:
Look at the night sky with an adult to see the different constellations. Choose a constellation that you would like to create or create your own star pattern. Have an adult use the pencil to punch holes in the bottom of the round cardboard container. Then, turn out the lights. Shine the flashlight into the open end of the cardboard container to make the star pattern appear on your ceiling or wall.

1. What is a constellation? _____

2. Which constellation did you make with your star pattern? If you created your own constellation, name it. _____

3. When can you see stars in the sky? _____

4. What else can you see in the night sky? _____
_____

5. Long ago, people told stories about constellations. On another sheet of paper, write a story or draw a picture that tells about your constellation.

BONUS

Science Experiment

Grasping Objects

How do your thumbs help you grasp objects?

Materials:
- tape
- pencil
- several small objects

Procedure:
Have an adult help you tape the thumb of your writing hand to your palm so that you cannot move it. The tape should allow your other fingers to move freely. Try to pick up a pencil and write your name. Then, try to tie your shoes. Next, try to pick up each small object.

Remove the tape. Repeat each activity. Notice how your thumb works as you complete each activity.

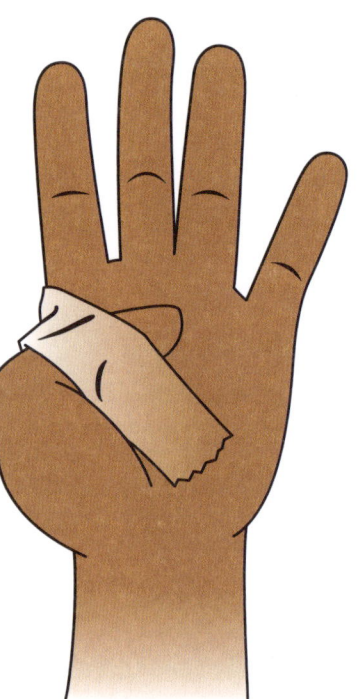

1. Circle the activity that was easier.

    A. writing with a taped hand

    B. writing with no tape on your hand

2. Circle the activity that was more difficult.

    A. tying your shoe with no tape on your hand

    B. tying your shoe with a taped hand

3. Circle the names of the animals who have thumbs that help them grasp objects.

    monkey   fish

    frog   gorilla

Science Activity

It's Only Natural!

Look at each object. Write *M* if the object is made by people. Write *N* if the object is natural (not made by people).

1.  _____

2.  _____

3.  _____

4.  _____

5. 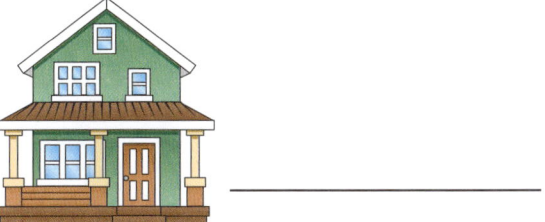 _____

6.  _____

7.  _____

8.  _____

9.  _____

10.  _____

Social Studies Activity

BONUS

Globe

Color the water blue. Color the land green. Have an adult help you find a map or a globe online or at a library to check your coloring.

Social Studies Activity

BONUS

Travel Today

Look at the wagon. In the past, people used horse-drawn wagons to travel long distances. Draw what we use to travel today.

PAST

PRESENT

BONUS

Outdoor Extension Activities

Take It Outside!

Go outside with an adult. Choose an object and place it on a hard surface. Use a piece of chalk to trace the outline of the object's shadow. Return to the object at a different time of day and trace the shadow again. What do you notice about the two shadows?

Go outside with an adult. Look for different places where animals make their homes, such as in trees or creeks. Make sure not to touch any animals or their homes! What kind of animal do you think lives in each home?

Go outside with an adult. Collect five leaves. Talk about the leaves with the adult. Are they the same color? Are they the same shape? Did they fall from trees or bushes? How are they alike, and how are they different? Use the Internet or a book from the library to identify the leaves. Photograph or draw a picture of the leaves and label them. If you would like to, send the drawings or photos to a friend or family member.

* See page ii.

SECTION III

Monthly Goals

Think of three goals that you would like to set for yourself this month. For example, you may want to learn three new words each week. Have an adult help you write your goals on the lines.

Place a sticker next to each of your goals that you complete. Feel proud that you have met your goals!

1. _____ [PLACE STICKER HERE]
2. _____ [PLACE STICKER HERE]
3. _____ [PLACE STICKER HERE]

Word List

The following words are used in this section. They are good words for you to know. Read each word aloud with an adult. When you see a word from this list on a page, circle it with your favorite color of crayon.

answers	family
clock	sentence
date	spell
dimes	time
equal	title

SECTION III

Introduction to Endurance

This section includes fitness and character development activities that focus on endurance. These activities are designed to get your child moving and to get her thinking about developing her physical and mental stamina. If your child has limited mobility, feel free to modify any suggested exercises to fit individual abilities.

Physical Endurance

Many children seem to have endless energy and can run, jump, and play for hours. But, other children may not have developed that kind of endurance. Improving endurance requires regular aerobic exercise, which causes the heart to beat faster and the person to breathe harder. As a result of regular aerobic activity, the heart becomes stronger, and the blood cells deliver oxygen to the body more efficiently. There are many ways for a child to get an aerobic workout that does not feel like exercise. Jumping rope and playing tag are examples.

Summer provides a variety of opportunities to bolster your child's endurance. If you see your child head for the TV, suggest an activity that will get her moving instead. Explain that while there are times when a relaxing indoor activity is valuable, it is important to take advantage of the warm mornings and sunny days to go outdoors. Reserve the less active times for when it is dark, too hot, or raining. Explain the importance of physical activity and invite her to join you for a walk, a bike ride, or a game of basketball.

Endurance and Character Development

Endurance applies to the mind as well as to the body. Explain to your child that *endurance* means to stick with something. Children can demonstrate mental endurance every day. For example, staying with a task when she might want to quit and keeping at it until it is done are ways that a child can show endurance.

Take advantage of summertime to help your child practice her mental endurance. Look for situations where she might seem frustrated or bored. Perhaps she asked to take swimming lessons, but after a few early-morning classes, she is not having as much fun as she had imagined. Turn this dilemma into a learning opportunity. It is important that children feel some ownership in decision making, so guide her to some key points to consider, such as how she asked all spring for permission to take lessons. Remind her that she has taken only a few lessons, so she might get used to the early-morning practices. Let her know that she has options to make the experience more enjoyable, such as going to bed earlier or sleeping a few extra minutes during the morning ride to lessons. Explain that quitting should be the last resort. Teaching your child at a young age to endure will help her as she continues to develop into a happy, healthy person.

Addition & Subtraction/Numbers & Counting

DAY 1

Add or subtract to solve each problem.

1. 2
   +3

2. 1
   +4

3. 5
   +2

4. 3
   +0

5. 3
   +4

6. 2
   −1

7. 8
   −6

8. 9
   −5

9. 4
   −3

10. 4
   −1

Write the missing numbers.

1	2								
					16				
		23							
								39	
			44						50

DAY 1

Grammar & Language Arts

A *verb* shows action. Look at the underlined verb in each sentence. If it tells what is happening right now, write *now* on the line. If it tells what already happened, write *past* on the line. If it tells what will happen in the future, write *future* on the line.

11. Maddy <u>stands</u> in the rain. _____

12. Gus <u>jumped</u> up and down. _____

13. I <u>will do</u> the dishes. _____

14. The baby <u>slept</u> all night. _____

15. Tasha <u>pets</u> the dog. _____

16. Mr. Garza <u>will bring</u> popcorn. _____

Use the words in the sentence to figure out the meaning of each underlined word. Circle your answer.

17. The <u>wee</u> mouse ran under the bush.

    A. tiny   B. huge

18. Grandpa caught two <u>flounder</u> when we went fishing.

    A. fish   B. birds

19. Tessa felt <u>anxious</u> about riding without training wheels.

    A. pretty   B. worried

20. Ivan's dog <u>bays</u> at the moon.

    A. smiles   B. howls

21. The <u>ancient</u> tree is more than 100 years old.

    A. very old   B. pine

Grammar & Language Arts/Numbers & Counting

DAY 2

Say the name of each picture. Write *1* if the word has one syllable. Write *2* if the word has two syllables.

1.
   _____

2.
   _____

3.
   _____

4.
   _____

Write the missing numbers.

51	52								
				65					
		73							
						87			
			94						100

101

© Carson Dellosa Education

DAY 2

Phonics

Say the name of each picture. Circle the pictures with the same beginning sound as the letter in each row.

5. f

6. c

7. d

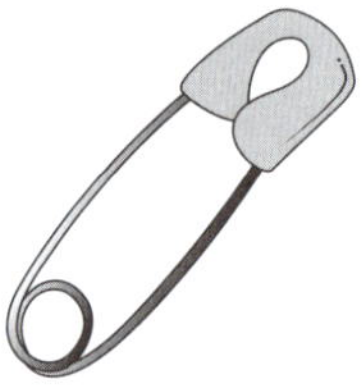

8. g

9. h

FITNESS FLASH: Do 10 jumping jacks.

* See page ii.

102

© Carson Dellosa Education

Reading Comprehension/Fitness

DAY 3

Read the story with an adult. Answer the questions.

Dark clouds gathered in the sky. A cool wind blew. The trees **swayed** back and forth. Gemma could hear a deep rumble close by. She flipped on a light. Her room filled with a warm glow. She pulled the fuzzy blanket around her. Then, she grabbed a book. Snug and happy, Gemma began to read.

1. How do you think Gemma feels?

    A. bored

    B. scared

    C. cozy

2. What does *swayed* mean?

    A. fell

    B. broke

    C. bent

3. Write three words from the story that helped paint a picture in your mind.

_____   _____   _____

Obstacle Course

Having endurance means that you can exercise harder and for longer amounts of time. The more you exercise, the easier it will be each time. Use this activity to improve your physical endurance.

Create an obstacle course with an adult. Use soft objects from around your home to create obstacles to run around, jump over, crawl through, or carry. As you build endurance, add new obstacles to the course. How many times in a row can you complete the obstacle course?

* See page ii.

DAY 3

Phonics

Say the name of each picture. Circle the pictures with the same beginning sound as the letter in each row.

4. s

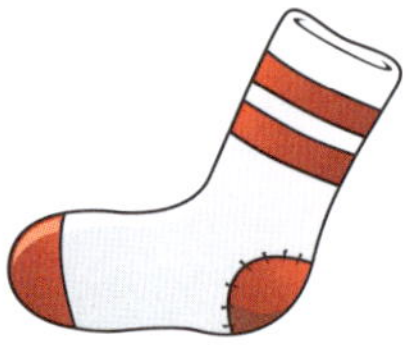

5. n

6. p

7. t

8. b

FACTOID: A human blinks at least 14,400 times a day.

© Carson Dellosa Education

Addition/Social Studies

DAY 4

Solve each problem.

1. Eddy's train has 2 green cars, 7 red cars, and 3 yellow cars. How many train cars does Eddy's train have in all?

2. Jada has 7 markers. She finds 3 more markers under her bed. Then, she finds 4 on her desk. How many markers does Jada have in all?

3. Bella picked 2 flowers one day. The next day, she picked 4. Today, she picked 3. How many flowers did she pick in all?

Think of a special holiday, custom, or tradition that your family observes. Draw and color a picture of your family celebrating the holiday. Write each person's name beside his or her picture.

DAY 4

Phonics

Say the name of each picture. Circle the pictures with the same beginning sound as the letter in each row.

4.	j	 baseball	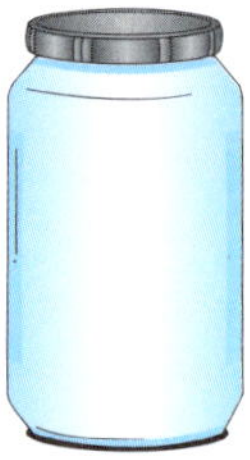 jar	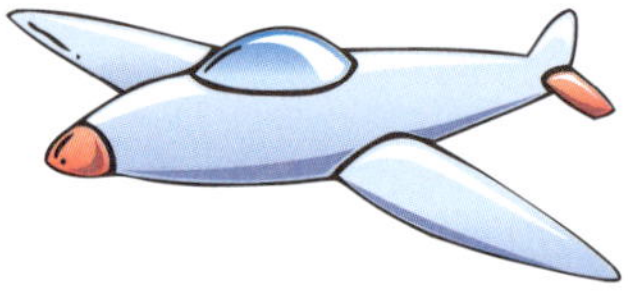 jet
5.	r	rabbit	horse	ring
6.	k	key	hat	kite
7.	w	web	apple	watch
8.	z	zebra	zipper	tent

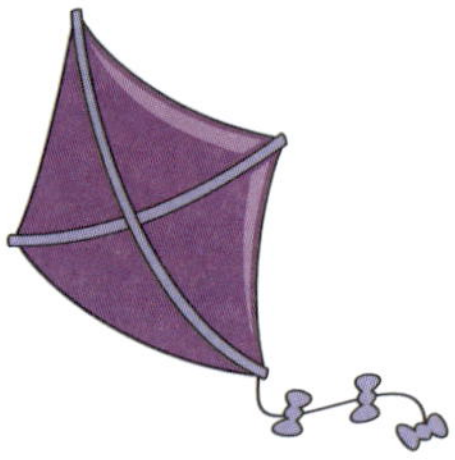

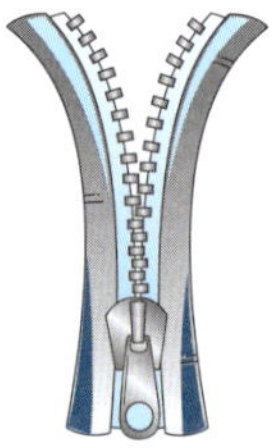

FITNESS FLASH: Jog in place for 30 seconds.

* See page ii.

106

© Carson Dellosa Education

Grammar & Language Arts

DAY 5

Look at each picture. Underline the word that completes the sentence.

1.  The fish are (between, in) the tank.

2.  The kite is (above, beside) the girl.

3.  The plate is (above, under) the cake.

4.  The boy is (beside, behind) the girl.

5.  Did you put the pillow (in, on) the bed?

Write words to describe each object.

ice cream

_____

_____

_____

_____

watermelon

_____

_____

_____

_____

DAY 5

Reading Comprehension

Read the story. Answer the questions.

Tasha the Zookeeper

Tasha is a zookeeper. Her job is to keep the animals safe and happy. She cleans the habitats and gives the animals food and water.

Last week, a hawk began to squawk. Tasha saw that he had a hurt wing. She called a vet to fix the hawk's wing. Later, she helped a lion with a sore paw. Soon, the lion was strong and **healthy**. Then, Tasha cleaned the bears' home. She hid a treat for the bears to find. Tasha enjoys her job.

6. Which sentence tells what the story is about?

    A. Tasha takes care of the animals at the zoo.

    B. Tasha is safe and happy.

    C. The animals like Tasha.

7. What happened to the hawk?

    A. The hawk could not sing.

    B. The hawk had a hurt wing.

    C. The hawk was hungry.

8. What does *healthy* mean?

    A. sick

    B. well

    C. weak

9. What does Tasha do at her job? _____

CHARACTER CHECK: Think of a time when you helped a friend or family member. How did helping make you feel? Draw a picture of how you helped.

Addition & Subtraction/Visual Discrimination

DAY 6

Solve each problem.

1. Zara picks 16 tulips. She puts 9 in a vase for Mom. How many are left?

2. Luke took out 11 books from the library. The next day, he returned 3. How many does he still have?

3. Danny bought 6 baseball cards. Dad gave him 4 more. Vinh gave him 6 more. How many does Danny have in all?

Draw a house to match the first house. Color the houses.

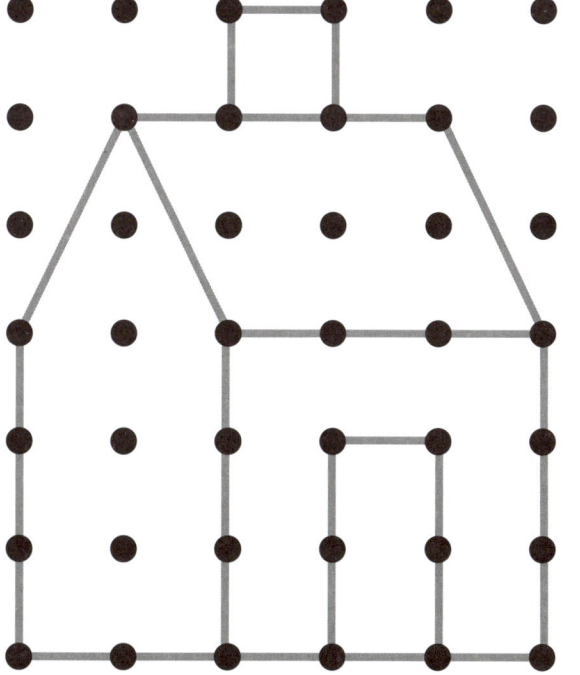

DAY 6

Phonics

Say the name of each picture. Write the letter of the beginning sound.
EXAMPLE:

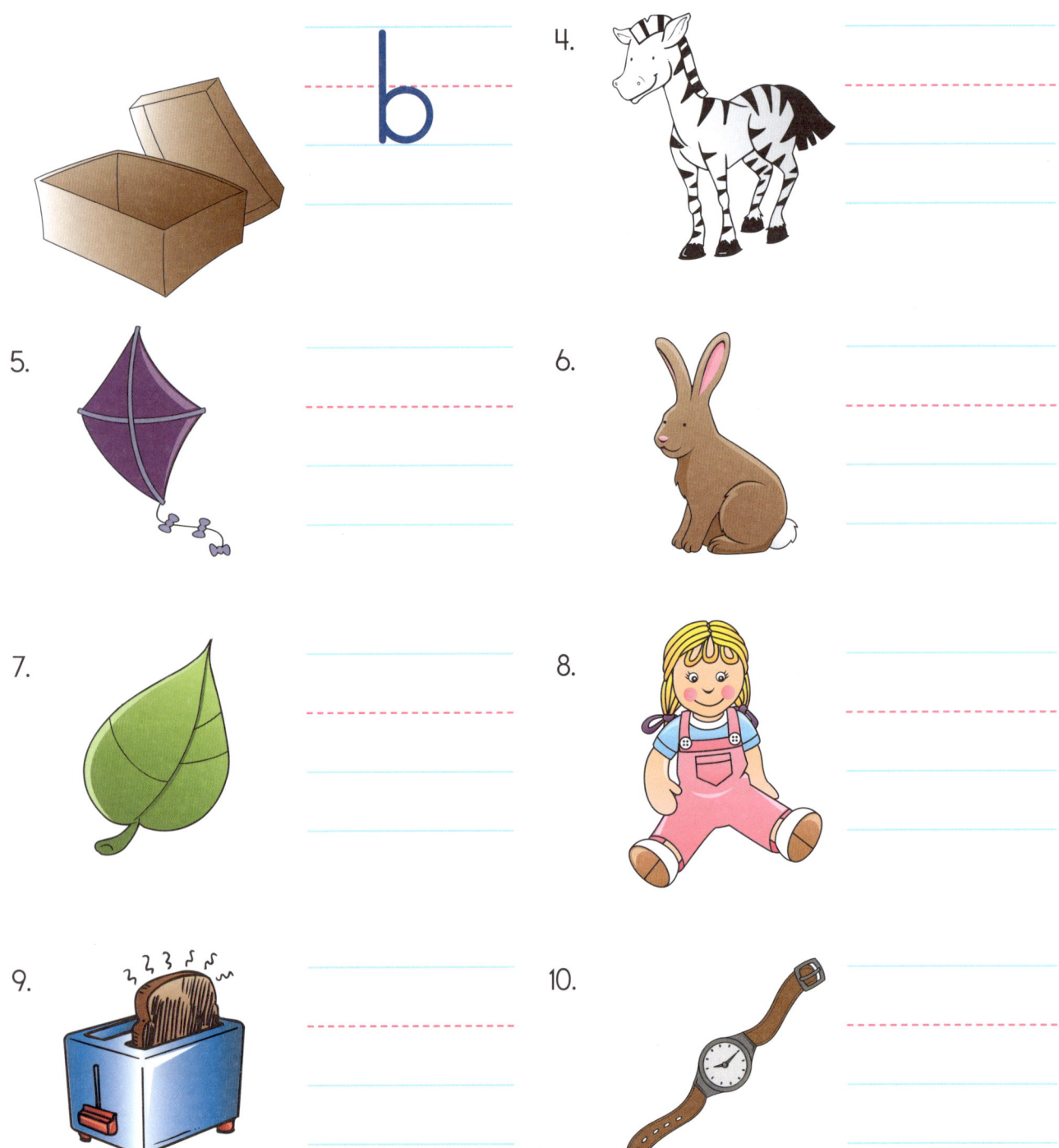

FACTOID: Australia's Great Barrier Reef can be seen from outer space.

Money/Subtraction

DAY 7

When you count dimes, you count by tens. Count each set of dimes. Write the total amount.

1.

_____ ¢

2.

_____ ¢

3.

_____ ¢

4.

_____ ¢

Solve each problem.

5. 30 − 10 = _____
6. 70 − 50 = _____
7. 100 − 40 = _____

8. 60 − 10 = _____
9. 80 − 30 = _____
10. 50 − 20 = _____

11. 90 − 50 = _____
12. 40 − 20 = _____
13. 60 − 40 = _____

DAY 7

Phonics

Say the name of each picture. Write the letter of the beginning sound.
EXAMPLE:

14.

15.

16.

17.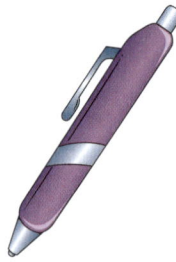

18.

19.

20.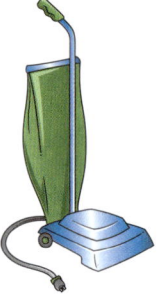

FITNESS FLASH: Hop on your right foot for 30 seconds.

* See page ii.

Addition/Grammar & Language Arts

DAY 8

Add to find each sum.

1. 5
   +3

2. 4
   +5

3. 9
   +1

4. 2
   +7

5. 3
   +4

6. 8
   +2

7. 9
   +0

8. 1
   +8

9. 5
   +5

10. 5
    +2

11. 6
    +2

12. 3
    +5

An *adjective* is a describing word. Write an adjective from the box to describe each word.

| green | fluffy | sticky | sour | hot |

_____ sun

_____ frog

_____ glue

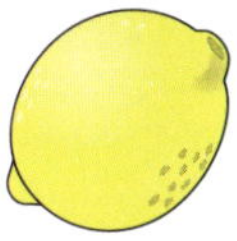

_____ lemon

_____ cat

DAY 8

Read the poem. Answer the questions.

Our Tree House

My friend and I are way up high,
watching as the world goes by,
in our tree house.

Down on the ground,
little people move around
below our tree house.

Birds fly above and below us.
They **screech** and make a loud fuss
around our tree house.

13. Who is in the tree house?

    A. two monkeys

    B. two friends

    C. two dogs

14. What does *screech* mean?

    A. to circle

    B. to make a loud sound

    C. to stand

15. Write four words from the poem that rhyme with *my*.

    _____ _____ _____ _____

16. Write another good title for the poem.

    _____

FACTOID: One of the largest wooden tree houses in the world has a restaurant and a gift shop inside it.

Addition/Geometry

DAY 9

Add to find each sum.

1. 6 + 2 = _____
2. 5 + 1 = _____
3. 4 + 3 = _____

4. 1 + 7 = _____
5. 2 + 8 = _____
6. 9 + 0 = _____

7. 3 + 5 = _____
8. 4 + 6 = _____
9. 7 + 2 = _____

10. 8 + 1 = _____
11. 1 + 9 = _____
12. 6 + 3 = _____

Draw a line to divide the circle into two equal halves.

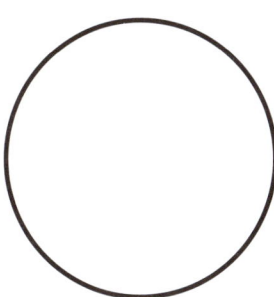

Draw lines to divide the square into four equal quarters.

Draw a line to divide the triangle into two equal halves.

Draw lines to divide the rectangle into four equal quarters.

DAY 9

Say the name of each picture. Circle the letter of the ending sound.

EXAMPLE:

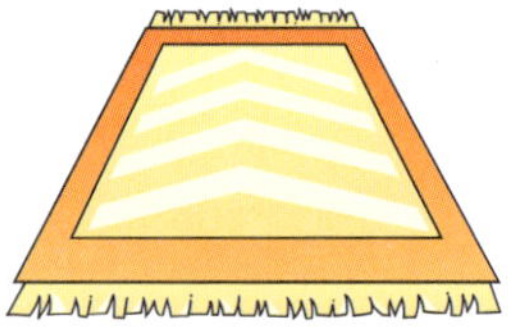

w (g) t

13.

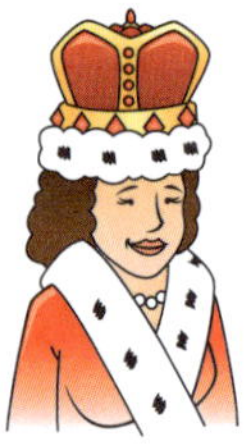

k n m

14.

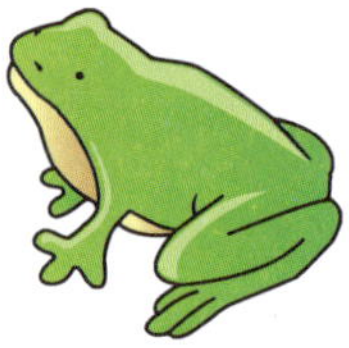

g d c

15.

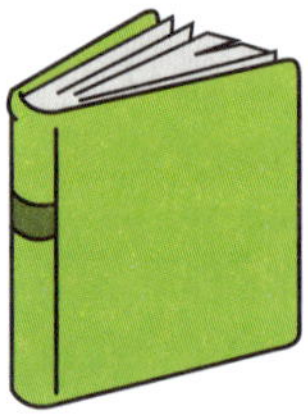

j k w

16.

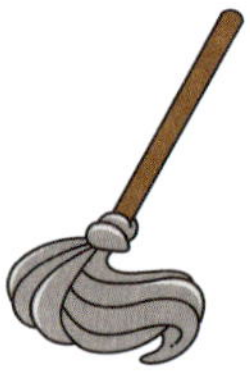

d p c

17.

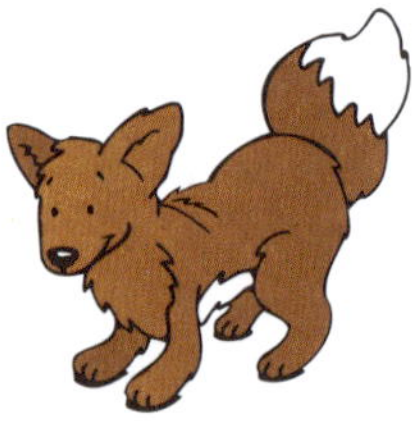

k f x

18.

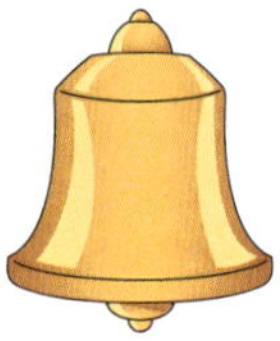

t l n

19.

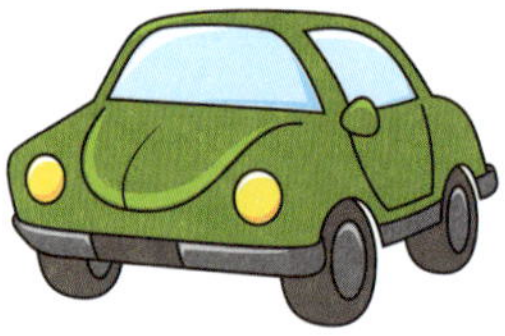

h r b

20.

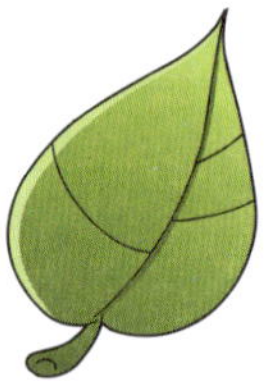

f t l

21.

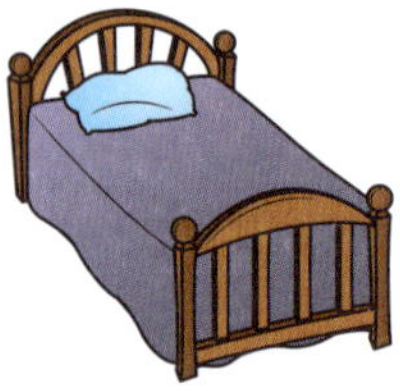

c d k

22.

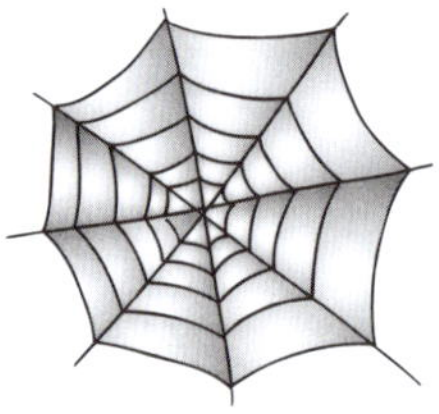

h j b

23.

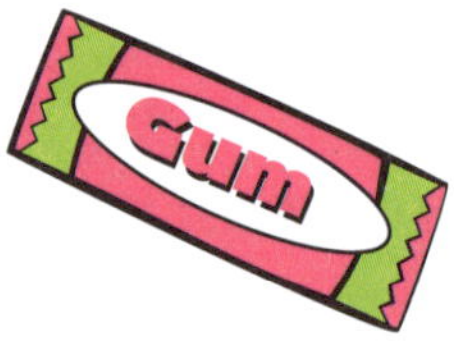

n m h

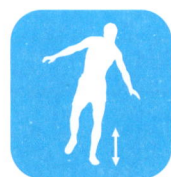

FITNESS FLASH: Hop on your left foot 10 times.

* See page ii.

PLACE STICKER HERE

Subtraction/Grammar & Language Arts

DAY 10

Subtract to find each difference.

1. 7
   −3

2. 8
   −5

3. 9
   −1

4. 6
   −2

5. 5
   −4

6. 8
   −3

7. 6
   −3

8. 8
   −7

9. 5
   −2

10. 7
    −5

11. 9
    −4

12. 8
    −6

A *conjunction* is a joining word. Choose the conjunction that completes each sentence. Write it on the line.

13. Ezra _____ Jack made some muffins.
    (and, but)

14. There are no swim lessons today _____ of the rain.
    (so, because)

15. Do you want green beans _____ salad?
    (or, but)

16. The baby is crying, _____ Mom will feed her.
    (or, so)

17. I like peanuts _____ not peanut butter.
    (but, because)

DAY 10

Read the story. Answer the questions.

The day was hot. I was bored. I wanted to swim.
"Mom, can we go to the pool?" I asked.
"Not right now, Ada," said Mom.
The park was cool. Lots of trees grew there. "Mom, can we go to the park?" I asked.
"Not right now, Ada," said Mom.
Inside was cool. A game inside would be fun. "Mom, can we play a game?"
"Not right now, Ada," said Mom.
I sat on my bed. I kicked my feet. I was still hot and bored. Then, I had a plan.
"Mom, can I make ice pops?"
"Sure," said Mom. "We have some fruit punch."
I made ice pops. They were cool. They were fruity. Yum!

18. What is the story mostly about?

    A. Lots of trees grow at the park.

    B. Ada wants to find something cool to do.

    C. Ada likes to play games.

19. Who is telling the story?

    A. Mom

    B. Ada

    C. Ada's friend

20. How does Ada solve her problem?

    _____

CHARACTER CHECK: Make a card for a friend or family member you have not seen in a long time. Ask an adult to help you mail your card.

Subtraction/Grammar & Language Arts

DAY 11

Subtract to find each difference.

1. 15 − 2 = _____
2. 19 − 3 = _____
3. 20 − 1 = _____
4. 17 − 4 = _____
5. 16 − 2 = _____
6. 18 − 5 = _____
7. 19 − 5 = _____
8. 20 − 2 = _____
9. 17 − 3 = _____
10. 18 − 4 = _____
11. 15 − 5 = _____
12. 16 − 3 = _____
13. 20 − 0 = _____
14. 16 − 4 = _____
15. 15 − 3 = _____

What are you an expert in? Do you know a lot about dogs or baseball? Maybe you are an expert in bugs, ballet, or fossils. Write a few sentences about something you know about. Ask an adult if you need help.

_____
_____
_____
_____
_____

DAY 11

Phonics

Say the name of each picture. Write the letters of the beginning and ending sounds.
EXAMPLE:

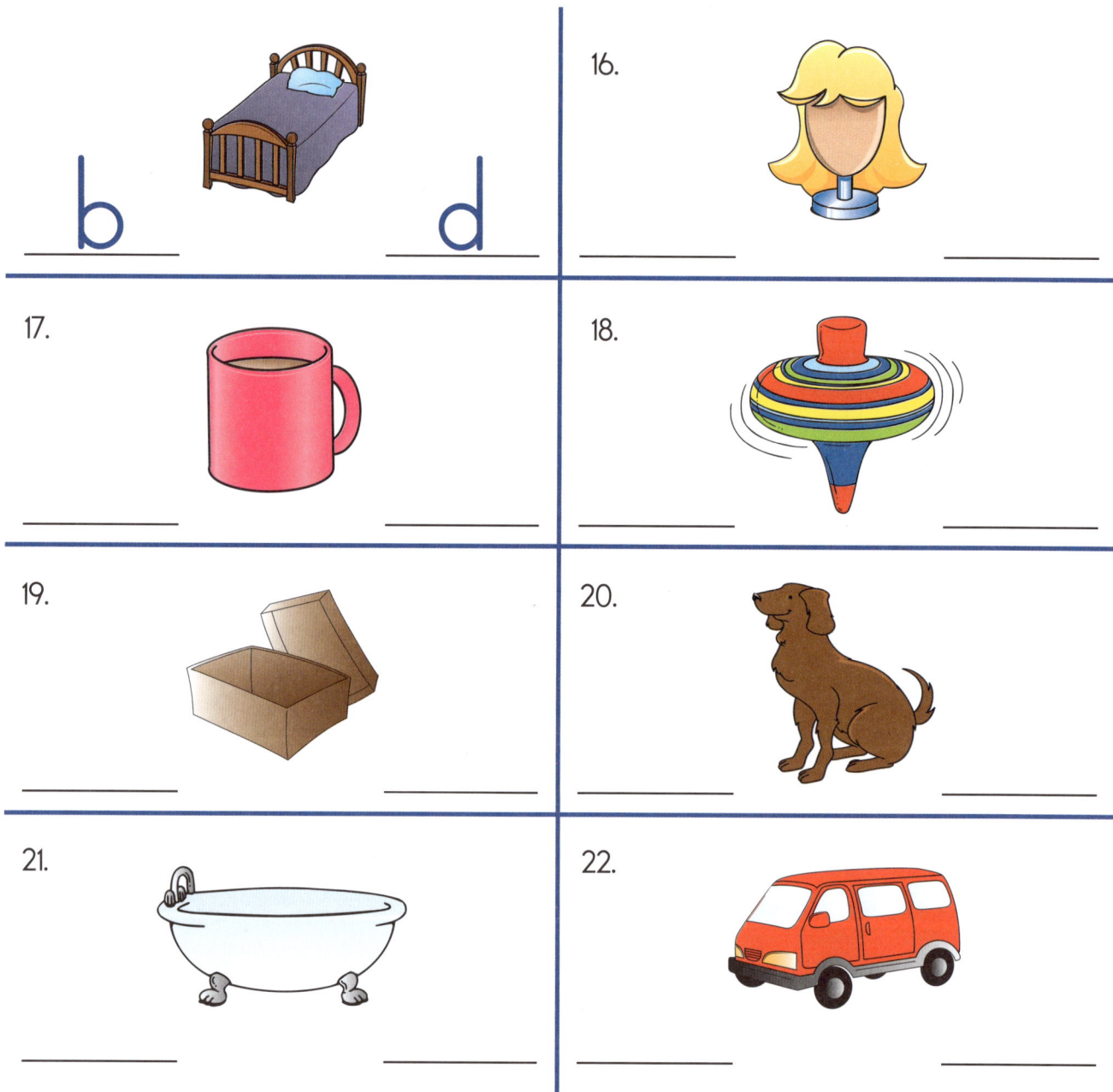

Addition & Subtraction/Phonics

DAY 12

Add or subtract to solve each problem.

1. 17
   + 3

2. 18
   − 2

3. 19
   − 5

4. 16
   + 2

5. 15
   + 3

6. 11
   + 8

7. 16
   − 3

8. 18
   − 7

9. 9
   +1

10. 17
    − 5

11. 19
    − 4

12. 18
    − 6

Say the name of each picture. Write the letters to complete each word.

13.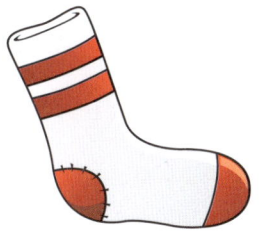
    so____ ____

14.
    ____ ____apes

15.
    fi____ ____

16.
    ____ ____irt

17.
    ____ ____ide

18.
    ki____ ____

DAY 12

Reading Comprehension

Read the story. Answer the questions.

Andre's Birthday

Andre's birthday was on Saturday. He had a very busy day.

In the morning, he went to breakfast with his grandmother. He had pancakes and juice. He ate all of the pancakes.

Then, Andre and six friends saw a movie. After the movie, they went back to Andre's house. They played tag and hide-and-seek.

Andre's dad fixed Andre his favorite meal for dinner. He made grilled cheese sandwiches and fruit salad. He also baked a cake with white icing. It was good!

19. On what day was Andre's birthday?

    A. Wednesday

    B. Friday

    C. Saturday

20. Whom did Andre go to breakfast with?

    A. his dad

    B. his grandmother

    C. his friends

21. What did Andre have for breakfast? _____

    _____

22. What did Andre and his friends do at Andre's house? _____

    _____

FITNESS FLASH: Hop on your right foot for 30 seconds.

* See page ii.

Numbers & Counting/Grammar & Language Arts

DAY 13

Write > (greater than) or < (less than) to compare each set of numbers.

1. 12 ◯ 22
2. 85 ◯ 41
3. 53 ◯ 19
4. 20 ◯ 13
5. 36 ◯ 59
6. 85 ◯ 55

When you write a date, a comma goes between the day and the year.

EXAMPLE: June 20, 1973

Read each date. Add commas where they are needed.

7. January 12 2015

8. May 3 2000

9. August 16 1967

10. February 27 2009

11. April 30 1984

12. October 1 2006

			June			
S	M	T	W	Th	F	S
						1
2	3	4	5	6	7	8
9	10	11	12	13	14	15
16	17	18	19	20	21	22
23	24	25	26	27	28	29
30						

DAY 13

Phonics

Say each word. Listen for the long *a* sound. Draw Xs on the two words that do not have the long *a* sound.

bake	cane	cage	tape
cake	lane	page	cape
tire	gate	rain	mane
ape	boat	pail	rake

Say the name of each picture. Write the letters you hear to spell each word.

13.
___ ___ ___ e

14.
___ ___ ___ e

15.
___ ___ ___ e

16.
___ ___ i ___

17.
___ ___ i ___

18.
___ ___ i ___ ___

FACTOID: The first Olympic Games were held in July 776 BC in Greece.

Addition & Subtraction

DAY 14

Add or subtract to solve each problem.

1. 19 – 3 = _____
2. 16 + 4 = _____
3. 15 + 3 = _____

4. 2 + 7 = _____
5. 18 – 2 = _____
6. 17 – 5 = _____

7. 14 + 5 = _____
8. 16 – 3 = _____
9. 16 + 3 = _____

10. 18 – 3 = _____
11. 19 – 4 = _____
12. 19 – 5 = _____

13. 15 + 4 = _____
14. 14 – 3 = _____
15. 17 + 2 = _____

Write a number sentence to solve each problem.

16.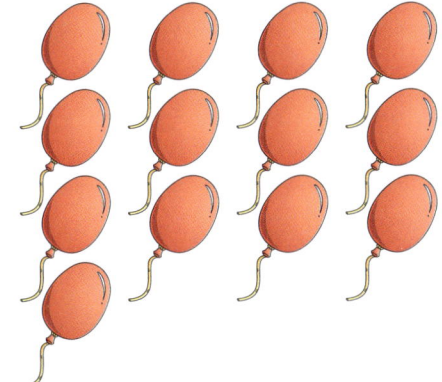

Thirteen balloons float in the air. One balloon pops. How many balloons are left?

_____ – _____ = _____

17.

Fifteen bees sat on flowers. Three bees flew away. How many bees are left?

_____ – _____ = _____

DAY 14

Phonics

Say each word. Listen for the long *e* sound. Draw Xs on the two words that do not have the long *e* sound.

eel	queen	feet	rose
feel	seed	sweet	beak
pea	bead	rake	beach
meal	bean	jeans	steam

Say the name of each picture. Write the letters you hear to spell each word.

18.

___ ___ ___ ___

19.

___ ___ ___ e

20.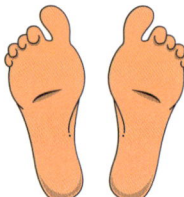

___ ___ ___ ___

21.

___ a ___ ___

22.

___ ___ a ___

23.

___ ___ a ___

 **FITNESS FLASH:** Do 10 jumping jacks.

*See page ii.

Addition & Subtraction/Character Development

DAY 15

Solve each pair of problems.

1. $9 - 6 =$ ☐

    $6 + $ ☐ $= 9$

2. $12 - 5 =$ ☐

    $5 + $ ☐ $= 12$

3. $15 - 5 =$ ☐

    $5 + $ ☐ $= 15$

4. $8 - 2 =$ ☐

    $2 + $ ☐ $= 8$

5. $17 - 10 =$ ☐

    $10 + $ ☐ $= 17$

6. $20 - 4 =$ ☐

    $4 + $ ☐ $= 20$

Perseverance Payoff

Perseverance means trying even if something is difficult to do. Have an adult help you write a list of situations in which you can show perseverance, such as learning a new math skill.

Make a second list. Have an adult help you write ways you can persevere through each situation. Make a third list that describes the rewards of persevering.

Remember that it is not always easy to persevere, but when you do, you will feel proud and happy about what you accomplished. When things get tough, do not give up. Imagine the benefits of always trying to do your best.

DAY 15

Phonics

Say each word. Listen for the long *i* sound. Draw Xs on the two words that do not have the long *i* sound.

pie	wide	ripe	like
tie	side	pipe	hike
life	cute	rise	mile
wife	tire	wise	seed

Say the name of each picture. Write the letters you hear to spell each word.

7.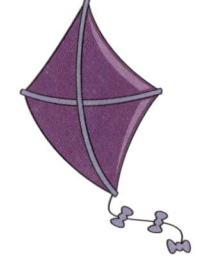
___ ___ ___ e

8.
___ ___ e

9.
___ ___ ___ e

10.
___ ___ e

11.
___ ___ ___ e

12.
___ ___ e

CHARACTER CHECK: What does it mean to be loyal?

Addition & Subtraction/Grammar & Language Arts

DAY 16

Add to find each sum.

1. 5
   +7

2. 12
   + 3

3. 3
   +7

4. 9
   +5

5. 15
   + 2

6. 13
   + 6

Subtract to find each difference.

7. 12
   − 8

8. 9
   −4

9. 15
   − 7

10. 8
    −8

11. 13
    − 3

12. 6
    −2

Read each sample sentence. Then, write your own sentence of the same type. Ask an adult if you need help.

Some sentences make statements.

I like to play the drums.

_____

Some sentences give commands.

Let the dog out.

_____

Some sentences ask questions.

Do you like plums?

_____

Some sentences express strong feelings.

Watch out for that vase!

_____

DAY 16

Phonics

Say each word. Listen for the long *o* sound. Draw Xs on the two words that do not have the long *o* sound.

hose	note	joke	bone
rose	page	poke	side
toad	boat	roast	goat
cone	toast	soap	soak

Say the name of each picture. Write the letters you hear to spell each word.

13.
___ a ___

14.
___ a ___

15.
___ ___ a ___ ___

16.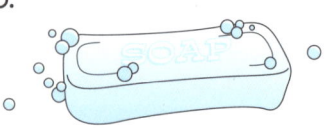
___ ___ a ___

17.
___ ___ ___ e

18.
___ ___ ___ e

FACTOID: A paleontologist is a scientist who studies fossils and dinosaur bones.

Measurement/Phonics

DAY 17

Find a small object you can use to measure things. It could be a pen, a paper clip, a toy car, or something else. Use it to measure each object below. Write your answer on the line.

I used _____ as a unit of measurement.

a shoe = _____

a windowsill = _____

a book = _____

a carton of milk or juice = _____

the kitchen sink = _____

Use the letters in the box to see how many words you can make. You will use each letter more than once.

> b m n p r s t

_p_ an   ___at   ___in

___an   ___at   ___in

___an   ___at   ___ug

___an   ___at   ___ug

___ut   ___et   ___op

___ut   ___et   ___op

DAY 17

Phonics

Say each word. Listen for the long *u* sound. Draw Xs on the two words that do not have the long *u* sound.

cute	tune	fume	unit
tire	mule	fuse	cube
beach	mute	tube	juice

Say the name of each picture. Write the letters you hear to spell each word.

1.

   ___ ___ ___ e

2.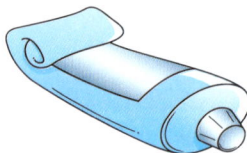

   ___ ___ ___ e

3.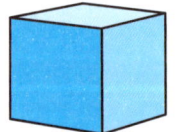

   ___ ___ ___ e

4.

   ___ ___ ___ ___ c

 **FITNESS FLASH:** Jog in place for 30 seconds.

* See page ii.

Addition/Grammar & Language Arts

DAY 18

Check the answers. Draw Xs on the boxes with incorrect sums. To solve the riddle, write the leftover letters in order on the answer lines.

1. 13 + 1 = 14 **w**	2. 12 + 2 = 20 **r**	3. 10 + 2 = 12 **a**	4. 11 + 4 = 14 **h**
5. 11 + 1 = 12 **v**	6. 11 + 2 = 14 **m**	7. 10 + 1 = 11 **e**	8. 14 + 1 = 15 **s**

How can you tell that the ocean is friendly?

It ____ ____ ____ ____ ____!

People have good days and bad days. Tell about a very good day or a very bad day you remember. Use complete sentences. Ask an adult if you need help.

_____

_____

_____

_____

_____

_____

_____

DAY 18

Reading Comprehension

Read the story. Answer the questions.

Twins

Sara and Sasha are twins. They like to do a lot of the same things. They both like to swim, jump rope, and ride bikes.

But, even twins like to do different things. Sara likes to play softball. Sasha likes to dance. In the winter, Sara likes to ice-skate. Sasha likes to go sledding. To help at home, Sara likes to set the table. Sasha likes to sweep the floor.

Both girls think that it is fun to have a twin.

9. Sara and Sasha are _____.

    A. twins

    B. friends

    C. teammates

10. Do the girls like being twins? _____

11. Draw a line to match each girl to the activities that she likes.

                                    ice-skating

    Sara   sweeping the floor

                                    sledding

    Sasha   dancing

                                    setting the table

                                    playing softball

FACTOID: Forty percent of twins invent their own language.

Time/Fitness

DAY 19

Look at each clock. Write the time shown.

1.

___ : ___

2.

___ : ___

3.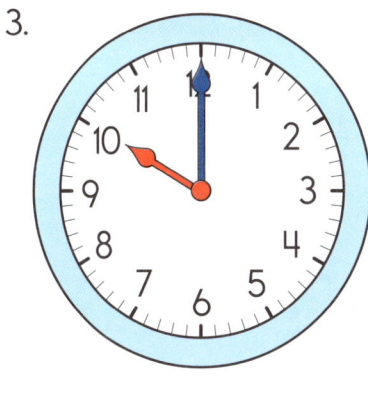

___ : ___

Read the time below each clock. Draw hands to show the correct time.

4.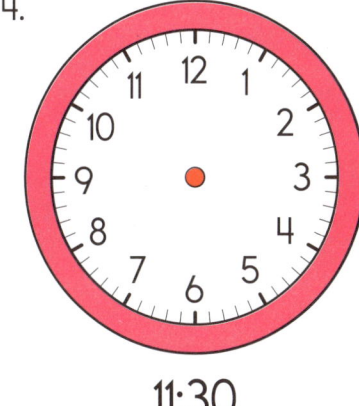

11:30

5.

6:00

6.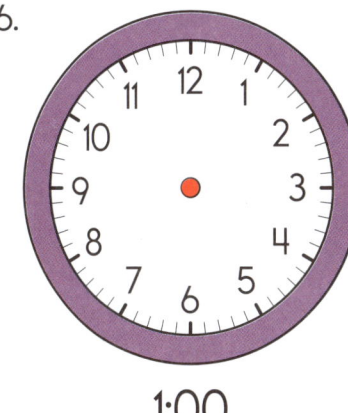

1:00

Pillowcase Race

Ask an adult if you may use an old pillowcase, pillows, and couch cushions. Use the soft objects to set up a winding course. Mark a turnaround spot so that you can retrace your hops to the start of the course.

Step into the pillowcase, and hop as fast as you can around the course. Ask an adult to time you. Set a goal, and repeat the course to try to beat your time. Keep trying until you reach your goal or show improvement.

* See page ii.

DAY 19

Phonics/Grammar & Language Arts

Say the name of each picture. Circle the two pictures in each row that have the same long vowel sound.

7.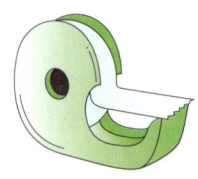

8.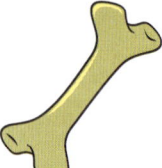

9.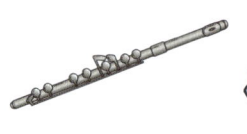

Number the pictures in the order in which they happened.

 **FITNESS FLASH:** Hop on your left foot 10 times.

* See page ii.

Measurement

DAY 20

Have an adult help you measure your height again. Fill in the blanks. Compare this measurement to your measurement on page 3. Then, draw and color the picture to look like you.

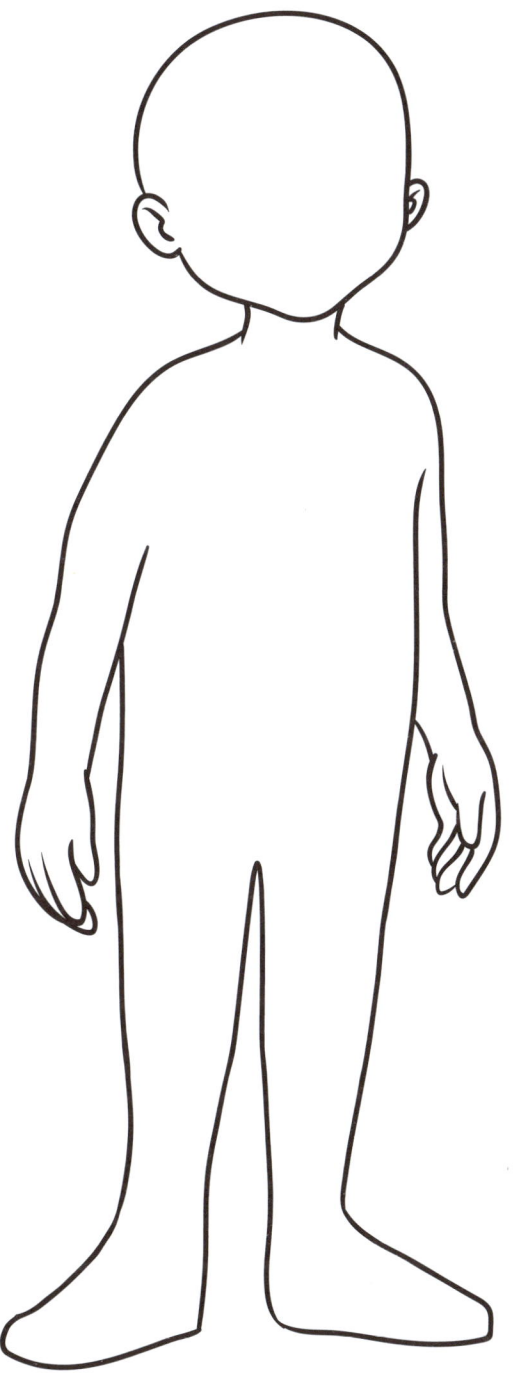

Your Height:

_____

How much have you grown this summer?

_____

DAY 20

Reading Comprehension

A *table of contents* tells you where to find things in a book. Use this table of contents to answer the questions. Circle the answers.

Table of Contents	
Where Frogs Live............4	Types of Frogs............16
What Frogs Eat............8	Ribbit! Frog Sounds............20
A Frog's Life Cycle............12	Look Out for Predators!............24

1. Turn to page _____ to find out about predators.
   A. 20
   B. 24
   C. 28

2. Turn to page _____ to find out what frogs eat.
   A. 8
   B. 16
   C. 20

3. Turn to page _____ to find out what kinds of sounds frogs make.
   A. 4
   B. 12
   C. 20

A *glossary* is found at the back of a book. It tells what certain words in the book mean. Use the glossary to answer the questions.

> **galaxy:** a group of many stars
> **Milky Way:** the galaxy that Earth is found in
> **solar system:** a sun and the planets that move around it
> **sun:** a star at the center of a solar system

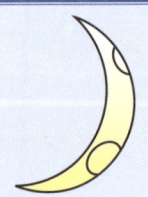

4. What is a galaxy? _____

5. What order are the words in the glossary in?
   A. number order
   B. ABC order
   C. no order

6. A sun and the planets that move around it are called
   A. a star
   B. a galaxy
   C. a solar system

Science Experiment

The Magic of Mulch

Does mulch (pine needles or leaves) help keep moisture in soil?

Materials:
- spade
- 2 plastic storage containers
- potting soil
- plastic cup
- water
- mulch

Procedure:

With an adult, use the spade to fill two plastic storage containers with the same amount of potting soil. Use the plastic cup to pour the same amount of water over the soil in each container. Feel the soil. Cover the soil in one container with mulch. Do not cover the soil in the second container. Place both containers in a sunny location. Feel the soil in each container every day for three days.

1. Which soil feels wetter on the third day? _____

   _____

2. Why is the soil in one container wetter than the soil in the other container? _____

   _____

3. How could a person keep the soil in her garden from drying out? _____

   _____

   _____

   _____

* See page ii.

BONUS

Science Experiment

Starting a New Tree

How do trees make more trees?

Materials:
- seeds from trees
- 2–3 disposable foam cups
- potting soil
- water
- notebook

Procedure:
Go outside with an adult. Collect seeds from trees such as maple, ash, pecan, and walnut. Have an adult help you add potting soil to each cup. Bury a few seeds in each cup. Water lightly. Place the cups on a windowsill. Water the soil regularly so that it is moist but not wet. Look each day for growing seedlings. Record the dates and your observations in the notebook.

1. If you continued to care for your seedlings, what would they grow into?

   _____

2. How do seeds move from one place to another? Circle all of the correct answers.

   A. Wind blows the seeds from one place to another.

   B. Seeds fall and stick to people and animals.

   C. The seeds walk themselves from one place to another.

   D. Rain moves the seeds from one place to another.

* See page ii.

Social Studies Activity

BONUS

Heroes

Who is your hero? Read about this person online. Answer the questions. Draw a picture of this person in the box.

Name:

Born in: _____

What do you like or admire about

this person? _____

_____

_____

_____

_____

What would you like to talk about with this person? _____

_____

_____

_____

_____

BONUS

Social Studies Activity

Road Signs

A person riding a bike must observe many road signs and signals in order to stay safe. Ask an adult to play the Road Signs game with you.

With an adult, find an example on the Internet of each road sign or signal in the chart below. Print the examples in a size that is large enough to easily be seen from a distance. Then, review the chart and printed examples. Begin the game when you are familiar with each sign or signal and the action associated with it.

Buckle your helmet securely for safety. When you are ready, ask an adult to display the "green light" signal. Pretend to ride your bike by holding imaginary handlebars while jogging forward.

The adult will display each traffic sign or signal. When the sign changes, perform its action from the chart. Remember to obey the speed limit and all traffic signs and signals. Otherwise, you might get a ticket!

Sign or Signal	Action
Green light	Jog slowly forward.
Left turn sign	Turn in circles to the left.
Left turn signal	Hold your left arm straight out. Then, turn to the left.
One way	Drive only in the direction in which the arrow points.
Red light	Come to a complete stop.
Right turn sign	Turn in circles to the right.
Right turn signal	Hold your left arm out in an *L* shape with your hand up. Then, turn to the right.
Slippery when wet	Slip and slide around the room.
Stop sign	Come to a complete stop.
Stop signal	Hold your left arm out in an *L* shape with your hand down. Then, stop.
Yield	Slow down and watch for other traffic.

* See page ii.

Social Studies Activity

BONUS

Mayflower Soap Ship

In September 1620, Pilgrims sailed from England across the Atlantic Ocean. They sailed on the *Mayflower* hoping to reach the New World. After landing in what is now the United States, they established the colony of Plymouth.

Materials:
- construction paper
- toothpicks
- floating bath soap
- water
- scissors
- tape
- sink

Procedure: Have an adult cut several rectangles from construction paper. Each rectangle should be about the same size as the bar of soap. These will be the sails. Tape a toothpick to each sail. Press each toothpick into the bar of soap to make a ship.

Fill the sink with water. Carefully place your boat in the water. Blow gently on the sails to move your ship across the water. Think about a new land that your ship could sail to.

Draw a picture of your ship.

Go to the library and look for a book about the *Mayflower*. See if you can find a picture of the ship. What can you learn about the Pilgrims' voyage by looking at the illustration?

BONUS

Outdoor Extension Activities

Take It Outside!

Decorate an empty shoe box to make a treasure chest. Fill the box with "treasure." Go outside with an adult and hide your treasure chest. Think of three clues about the location of the treasure chest. See if a friend or family member can follow your clues to find the treasure chest. Remember to bring your treasure chest inside at the end of the day so it does not get damaged.

Look around your house and list in a notebook five colors that you see. Go outside with an adult. Take your list with you and find items that match the colors on your list. Write the names of the items next to their colors.

Go outside with an adult during a rain shower. Stand under an overhang. Watch the raindrops hit the ground. What shapes do raindrops make when they hit the ground? What else do you notice about the falling rain? Write or draw your observations in a notebook or sketchbook.

* See page ii.

ANSWER KEY

Section 1

Day 2/Page 5: Students should trace and write the numbers.; 1. hat, rat; 2. can, pan; 3. top, mop

Students should practice writing the letter *B*.; Students should circle the book, bell, and butterfly.

Day 3/Page 7: Students should trace and write the numbers.; Students should circle the square, triangle, circle, hexagon, and rectangle. Students should underline the cone, cube, sphere, and cylinder.

Students should practice writing the letter *C*.; Students should circle the can, cat, car, and carrot.

Day 4/Page 9: Students should trace and write the numbers.; 1. 9; 2. 4; 3. 16; 4. 20

Students should practice writing the letter *D*.; Students should circle the doll, desk, dime, and dog.

Day 5/Page 11: 1. Possible answer: 5 + 5 = 10; 2. 10 – 3 = 7, 3. 10 – 6 = 4; 4. 10 + 4 = 14

Students should practice writing the letter *F*.; Students should circle the fence, fire truck, feather, and fan.

Day 6/Page 13:

Students should write the following lowercase letters: c, d, f, h, j, l, m, p, r, s, t, w, x, y.

Students should practice writing the letter *G*.; Students should circle the gum, goat, guitar, and gate.

Day 7/Page 15: 1. 6; 2. 7; 3. 8; 4. 10; Students should write the following uppercase letters: C, D, F, G, I, J, K, L, N, O, P, R, T, U, V, X, Y.

Students should practice writing the letter *H*.; Students should circle the house, hand, hat, and helicopter.

Day 8/Page 17: 1.–4. Students should draw the correct number of shapes.; 5. 10; 6. 11; 7. 13; 8. 14; 9. 12; 10. 15

Students should practice writing the letter *J*.; Students should circle the jar, jet, jack-o'-lantern, and jelly beans.

Day 9/Page 19: 1. 7; 2. 9; 3. 4; 4. 10; 5. 8; 6. 0; 7. 2; 8. 1; 9. 0; 10. 4; Students should match each uppercase letter to its lowercase letter.

Students should practice writing the letter *K*.; Students should circle the king, key, kite, and koala.

Day 10/Page 21: 1. 2; 2. 1; 3. 2; Students should match each uppercase letter to its lowercase letter.

Students should practice writing the letter *L*.; Students should circle the ladder, lamp, leaf, and lemon.

Day 11/Page 23: Students should circle these items in red: shoe, dress, and vest.; Students should circle these items in green: plum, apple, cheese, and sandwich.; 1. 4; 2. 3; Students should complete the graph as shown:

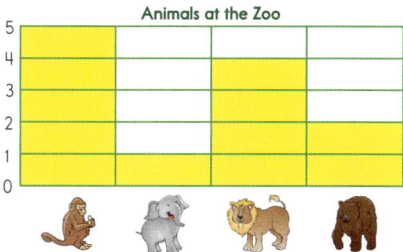

3. monkeys

Students should practice writing the letter *M*.; Students should circle the mop, monkey, mailbox, and mitten.

Day 12/Page 25: 11; 12; 13; 14; 15; 16; 17; 18; 19; 1. 4 + 6 = 10; 4 + 6 = 10; 10 – 4 = 6; 10 – 6 = 4; 2. 7 + 3 = 10; 3 + 7 = 10; 10 – 3 = 7; 10 – 3 = 7

Students should practice writing the letter *N*.; Students should circle the net, nuts, notebook, and nine.

ANSWER KEY

Day 13/Page 27: 1 apple, 2 oranges, 3 lemons, 4 balloons, 5 balls. Students should circle the girl and the baby. Students should draw Xs on the school and the farm. Students should draw squares around the pencil and the desk.

Students should practice writing the letter *P*.; Students should circle the penguin, pumpkin, pencil, and piano.

Day 14/Page 29: 1. Students should circle the top-right fishbowl.; 2. Students should circle the top-right plate.; 3. ring; 4. tail; 5. map

Students should practice writing the letter *Q*.; Students should circle the quilt, question mark, quail, and quarter.

Day 15/Page 31: Students should circle the following sets: 1. five strawberries; 2. two apples.

Students should practice writing the letter *R*.; Students should circle the rocket, rabbit, ring, and rainbow.

Day 16/Page 33: Students should complete the graph as shown:

1	2	3	4	5
6	7	8	9	10
11	12	13	14	15
16	17	18	19	20
21	22	23	24	25

box, fox; top, mop; frog, log; pan, fan

Students should practice writing the letter *S*.; Students should circle the sock, seal, soap, sun, and saw.

Day 17/Page 35: 1. tape; 2. mop; 3. slide; 4. ?; 5. .; 6. ?; 7. !; 8. .; 9.?; 10.!

Students should practice writing the letter *T*.; Students should circle the tiger, tent, top, and turtle.

Day 18/Page 37: 1. planted; 2. darker; 3. unhappy; 4. playful; 5. refill; 6. preheat; 7. – 9. Answers will vary.

Students should practice writing the letter *V*.; Students should circle the vase, van, vest, and violin.

Day 19/Page 39: 1. bees; 2. hats; 3. kites; 4. socks.; 5. see; 6. my; 7. and; 8. The; 9. is; 10. at

Students should practice writing the letter *W*.; Students should circle the window, watermelon, watch, and wagon.

Day 20/Page 41: 1. What; 2. Who; 3. Where; 4. Why; 5. When

Students should practice writing the letter *X*.; Students should circle the ox, box, X-ray, and six.

Bonus Page 43: 1.–3. Answers will vary.

Bonus Page 44: 1. A; 2. B; 3. Answers will vary.; 4. The fan evaporates the water on the towel.

Bonus Page 45: Students should circle the first and third pictures. Drawings will vary.

Bonus Page 46: Students should circle the cell phone, jet, TV, laptop computer, and car.

Bonus Page 47:

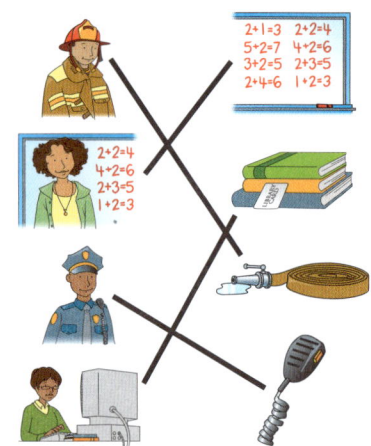

Section II

Day 1/Page 51: 1. 2; 2. 4; 3. 3; 4. 4; 5. 3; 6. 5; 7. 4; 8. 5; 9. Amad; 10. the park; 11. C

Students should practice writing the letter *Y*.; Students should circle the yogurt, yolk, yak, and yarn.

Day 2/Page 53: 1. 5; 2. 6; 3. 5; 4. 6; 5. 2; 6. 5; 7. 4; 8. 7; 9. 6; 10. 3

Students should practice writing the letter *Z*.; Students should circle the zipper, zebra, and zero.

Day 3/Page 55: 1. 4; 2. 5; 3. 3; 4. 4; 5. 4; 6. 5; Students should color the following number of boxes; horse–1; goat–2; sheep–3; rooster–5; cat–6; 7. cats; 8. 5

Students should practice writing the letter *A*.; Students should circle the apple, pan, hand, and hat.

Day 4/Page 57:

ANSWER KEY

72; 120; 30

4. fan; 5. cat; 6. map; 7. van; 8. cap; Students should draw an X on the word *bed*.

Day 5/Page 59: 1. a tree; 2. a bone; 3. 5

Students should underline each of the following words each time it is used: Sam, has, cat, Sam's, Max, cap, lap, bag, naps.; 4. A; 5. B; 6. A

Day 6/Page 61: 1. 1; 2. 1; 3. 3; 4. 3; 5. 2; 6. 0; 7. 1; 8. 2; 9. C, P; 10. P, C; 11. P, C; 12. C, P

Students should practice writing the letter *E*.; Students should circle the elephant, tent, bed, nest, and bell.

Day 7/Page 63: 1. 4; 2. 4; 3. 3; 4. 0; 5. 1; 6. 2; 7. 1; 8. 0; 9. 5; 10. 3; 11. X; 12. S; 13. X; 14. S; 15. S

16. tent; 17. pen; 18. vest; 19. egg; 20. nest; Students should draw an X on the word *bag*.

Day 8/Page 65: 1. 2; 2. 1; 3. 2; 4. 3; 5. 1; 6. 2; 9:00; 5:00; 2:00; 3:30; 9:30; 5:30

Students should underline each of the following words each time it is used: Meg, vet, vets, help, pets, get, well, leg, mend, head, pep, pet; 7. B; 8. pets; 9. T, T, F

Day 9/Page 67: 1. 4; 2. 1; 3. 5; 4. 2; 5. 1; 6. 0; 7. 3; 8. 0; 9. 4; 10. 1; Students should circle the taller boy, the fuller cup, the darker cat, and the smaller ball.

Students should practice writing the letter *I*.; Students should circle the wig, ring, pin, bib, and fish.

Day 10/Page 69: Students should circle the numbers as shown:

12	21	⟨12⟩	15	⟨12⟩	51	⟨12⟩	21	⟨12⟩
96	⟨96⟩	99	66	86	⟨96⟩	66	⟨96⟩	⟨96⟩
54	55	⟨54⟩	45	43	⟨54⟩	45	⟨54⟩	52
71	⟨71⟩	17	⟨71⟩	11	⟨71⟩	⟨71⟩	17	⟨71⟩
35	53	55	⟨35⟩	⟨35⟩	33	⟨35⟩	53	⟨35⟩

1. 20; 40; 2. 75; 95; 3. 32; 52; 4. 60; 80

5. sink; 6. milk; 7. bib; 8. ship; 9. six; Students should draw an X on the word *bug*.

Day 11/Page 71: 1. 20; 2. 40; 3. 30; 4. 50; 5. 10; 6. 60; Students should draw a triangle, rhombus, circle, oval, and rectangle.

Students should practice writing the letter *O*.; Students should circle the lock, clock, sock, and frog.

Day 12/Page 73: 1. 5 + 3 = 8, 5 + 3 = 8, 8 − 5 = 3, 8 − 3 = 5; 2. 8 + 2 = 10, 2 + 8 = 10; 10 − 8 = 2, 10 − 2 = 8; 3. 2 + 3 = 5; 3 + 2 = 5; 5 − 2 = 3; 5 − 3 = 2; Students should draw a line under the eraser. Students should circle the pencil.

4. clock; 5. lock; 6. sock; 7. top; 8. rock; Students should draw an X on the word *bib*.

Day 13/Page 75: 1. Students should circle the sandwich on the left.; 2. Students should circle the middle carrot.; 3. Students should circle the bean on the right.; 4. Students should circle the top-right eraser.; Students should circle the equations for #6, 7, 10, 12, and 13. Students should draw an X through the equations for #5, 8, 9, 11, and 14.

Students should underline each of the following words each time it is used: frog, on, log, pond, along, dog, Rob, song, hopped, off, fox, popped.; 15. Rob the dog; 16. C; 17. It hopped.; 18. It popped.; 19. Answers will vary.

Day 14/Page 77: 1. 18¢; 2. 15 stamps; 3. 8 comic books; 4. 11 balloons; Students should draw a line from 16 to the cabbages. Students should draw a line from 18 to the baseballs. Students should draw a line from 20 to the party horns.

Students should practice writing the letter *U*.; Students should circle the duck, mug, rug, and bus.

Day 15/Page 79: 1. ball; 2. book; 3. pumpkin; 4. shoe; Students should complete the crossword puzzles as shown:

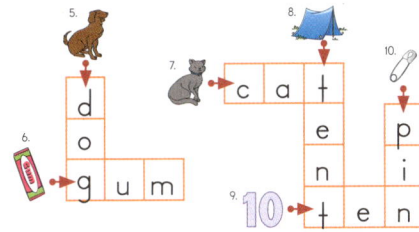

11. rug; 12. duck; 13. sun; 14. tub; 15. mug; Students should draw an X on the word *hat*.

Day 16/Page 81: 1. Students should circle the pitcher.; 2. Students should circle the gift on the left.; 3. Students should circle the box on the right.; 4. Students should circle the vase on the right.; Students should match the pictures as shown:

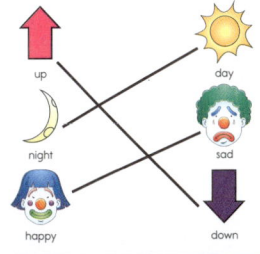

147

© Carson Dellosa Education

ANSWER KEY

Answers may vary. Possible answers: 5. her; 6. it; 7. I; 8. they; 9. him; 10. We; 11. sh; 12. ch; 13. wh; 14. sh; 15. ch

Day 17/Page 83: 1. S; 2. L; 3. S; 4. S; 5. L; 6. L; 7. L; 8. S

9. e/e; 10. i/o; 11. i; 12. e; 13. a/i; Students' writing will vary.

Day 18/Page 85: 1. B; 2. C; 3. nonfiction

Students should draw a line from tree to ee. Students should draw a line from kite to i_e. Students should draw a line from goat to oa. Students should draw a line from cake to a_e.; Rectangle = 4, 4; Triangle = 3, 3; Circle = 0, 0; Rhombus = 4, 4; Square = 4, 4; Trapezoid = 4, 4

Day 19 /Page 87: Students should touch and say each number.

1.swims; 2. jump; 3. falls; 4. are; 5. – 8. Students should check the following sentences: Carlos and Ben will meet us soon.; Mr. Chen lives on my block.; Kate, Lena, and Yoshi ate all the peaches.; I think Zack can cross the monkey bars.

Day 20/Page 89: Students should skip-count to connect the following numbers: 1. 0, 2, 4, 6, 8, 10; 2. 12, 14, 16, 18, 20, 22; 3. Wednesday; 4. Thursday; 5. July 8; 6.Friday

1; 1; 3; 2; 2; 3; 2; 1, 3; read; short; cloud; lick; grape; jump

Bonus Page 91: 1. a group of stars that make up a pattern; 2. Answers will vary.; 3. at night; 4. Answers will vary but may include: other planets, the moon, man-made satellites, and comets.; 5. Stories and pictures will vary.

Bonus Page 92: 1. B; 2. B; 3. monkey, gorilla

Bonus Page 93: 1. N; 2. N; 3. M; 4. N; 5. M; 6. M; 7. N; 8. M; 9. M; 10. M

Bonus Page 94: The globe should be colored as shown:

Bonus Page 95: Drawings will vary.

Section III

Day 1/Page 99: 1. 5; 2. 5; 3. 7; 4. 3; 5. 7; 6. 1; 7. 2; 8. 4; 9. 1; 10. 3; Students should complete the table as shown:

1	2	3	4	5	6	7	8	9	10
11	12	13	14	15	16	17	18	19	20
21	22	23	24	25	26	27	28	29	30
31	32	33	34	35	36	37	38	39	40
41	42	43	44	45	46	47	48	49	50

11. now; 12. past; 13. future; 14. past; 15. now; 16. future; 17; A; 18; A; 19. B; 20. B; 21. A

Day 2/Page 101: 1. 2; 2. 1; 3. 1; 4. 2; Students should complete the table as shown:

51	52	53	54	55	56	57	58	59	60
61	62	63	64	65	66	67	68	69	70
71	72	73	74	75	76	77	78	79	80
81	82	83	84	85	86	87	88	89	90
91	92	93	94	95	96	97	98	99	100

5. fish, feather; 6. camera, cake; 7. desk, dog; 8. goat, guitar; 9. hat, hammer

Day 3/Page 103: 1. C; 2. C; 3. Answers will vary. Possible answers: rumble, glow, fuzzy

4. seal, sock; 5. net, nail; 6. pear, pie; 7. tent, turtle; 8. bell, bed

Day 4/Page 105: 1. 12 cars; 2. 14 markers; 3. 9 flowers; Drawings will vary.

4. jar, jet; 5. rabbit, ring; 6. key, kite; 7. web, watch; 8. zebra, zipper

Day 5/Page 107: 1. in; 2. above; 3. under; 4. beside; 5. on; Describing words will vary.

6. A; 7. B; 8. B; 9. She keeps the animals safe and happy. She cleans the habitats and gives the animals food and water.

Day 6/Page 109: 1. 7 tulips; 2. 8 books; 3. 16 baseball cards; Students should draw a house and color both pictures.

4. z; 5. k; 6. r; 7. l; 8. d; 9. t; 10. w

Day 7/Page 111: 1. 20; 2. 60; 3. 30; 4. 40; 5. 20; 6. 20; 7. 60; 8. 50; 9. 50; 10. 30; 11. 40; 12. 20; 13. 20

14. s; 15. d; 16. f; 17. p; 18. l; 19. y; 20. v

Day 8/Page 113: 1. 8; 2. 9; 3. 10; 4. 9; 5. 7; 6. 10; 7. 9; 8. 9; 9. 10; 10. 7; 11. 8; 12. 8; hot; green; sticky; sour; fluffy

13. B; 14. B; 15. I, high, fly, by; 16. Answers will vary.

Day 9/Page 115: 1. 8; 2. 6; 3. 7; 4. 8; 5. 10; 6. 9; 7. 8; 8. 10; 9. 9; 10. 9; 11. 10; 12. 9;

ANSWER KEY

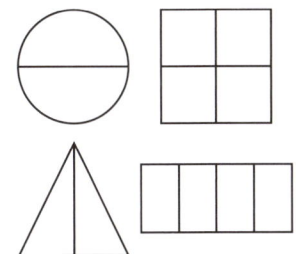

13. n; 14. g; 15. k; 16. p; 17. x; 18. l; 19. r; 20. f; 21. d; 22. b; 23. m

Day 10/Page 117: 1. 4; 2. 3; 3. 8; 4. 4; 5. 1; 6. 5; 7. 3; 8. 1; 9. 3; 10. 2; 11. 5; 12. 2; 13. and; 14. because; 15. or; 16. so; 17. but

18. B; 19. B; 20. Ada makes ice pops.

Day 11/Page 119: 1. 13; 2. 16; 3. 19; 4. 13; 5. 14; 6. 13; 7. 14; 8. 18; 9. 14; 10. 14; 11. 10; 12. 13; 13. 20; 14. 12; 15. 12; Students' writing will vary.

16. w, g; 17. m, g; 18. t, p; 19. b, x; 20. d, g; 21. t or b, b; 22. v, n

Day 12/Page 121: 1. 20; 2. 16; 3. 14; 4. 18; 5. 18; 6. 19; 7. 13; 8. 11; 9. 10; 10. 12; 11. 15; 12. 12; 13. ck; 14. gr; 15. sh; 16. sh; 17. sl; 18. ng

19. C; 20. B; 21. pancakes and juice; 22. played tag and hide-and-seek

Day 13/Page 123: 1. <; 2. >; 3. >; 4. >; 5. <; 6. >; 7. January 12, 2015; 8. May 3, 2000; 9. August 16, 1967; 10. February 27, 2009; 11. April 30, 1984; 12. October 1, 2006

Students should draw Xs on the words *tire* and *boat*.; 13. cake; 14. tape; 15. vase; 16. nail; 17. rain; 18. paint or pails

Day 14/Page 125: 1. 16; 2. 20; 3. 18; 4. 9; 5. 16; 6. 12; 7. 19; 8. 13; 9. 19; 10. 15; 11. 15; 12. 14; 13. 19; 14. 11; 15. 19; 16. 13 − 1 = 12; 17. 15 − 3 = 12

Students should draw Xs on the words *rose* and *rake*.; 18. tree; 19. three; 20. feet; 21. peach; 22. leaf; 23. peas

Day 15/Page 127: 1. 3, 3; 2. 7, 7; 3. 10, 10; 4. 6, 6; 5. 7, 7; 6. 16, 16

Students should draw Xs on the words *cute* and *seed*.; 7. kite; 8. pie; 9. slide; 10. five; 11. bike; 12. nine

Day 16/Page 129: 1. 12; 2. 15; 3. 10; 4. 14; 5. 17; 6. 19; 7. 4; 8. 5; 9. 8; 10. 0; 11. 10; 12. 4; Sentences will vary.

Students should draw Xs on the words *page* and *side*.; 13. boat; 14. goat; 15. toast; 16. soap; 17. note; 18. rose

Day 17/Page 131: Answers will vary.; Answers will vary but may include: ran, tan, man, rut, but, put, nut, rat, sat, bat, mat, pat, set, bet, pet, net, tin, bin, pin, rug, tug, bug, mug, top, mop, pop.

Students should draw Xs on the words *tire* and *beach*.; 1. mule; 2. tube; 3. cube; 4. music

Day 18/Page 133: Students should draw an X on the following problems: 2, 4, and 6. It waves!; Students' writing will vary.

9. A; 10. yes; 11. Sara–ice skating, setting the table, playing softball; Sasha– sweeping the floor, sledding, dancing

Day 19/Page 135: 1. 2:00; 2. 4:30; 3. 10:00; 4.–6. Students should complete the clocks as shown:

7. tree, bee; 8. goat, bone; 9. vase, cake; 1, 3, 2, 4

Day 20/Page 138: Answers and drawings will vary.; 1. B; 2. A; 3. C; 4. a group of many stars; 5. B; 6. C

Bonus Page 139:
1. The one with the mulch feels wetter.; 2. The mulch kept the soil from drying out.; 3. She could cover the soil with mulch.

Bonus Page 140: 1. trees; 2. A, B, D

Bonus Page 141: Answers and drawings will vary.

Bonus Page 143: Drawings will vary.

NOTES

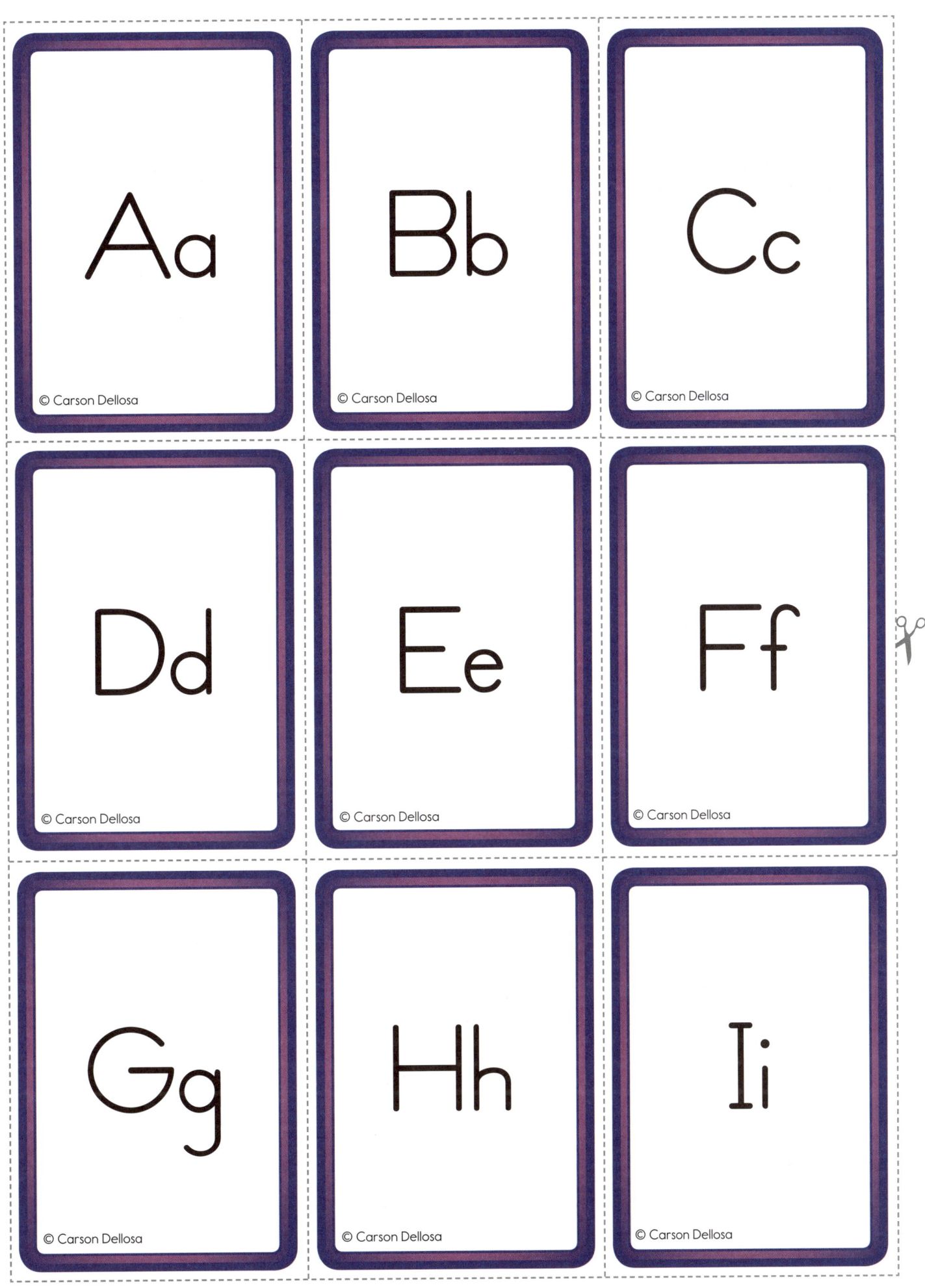

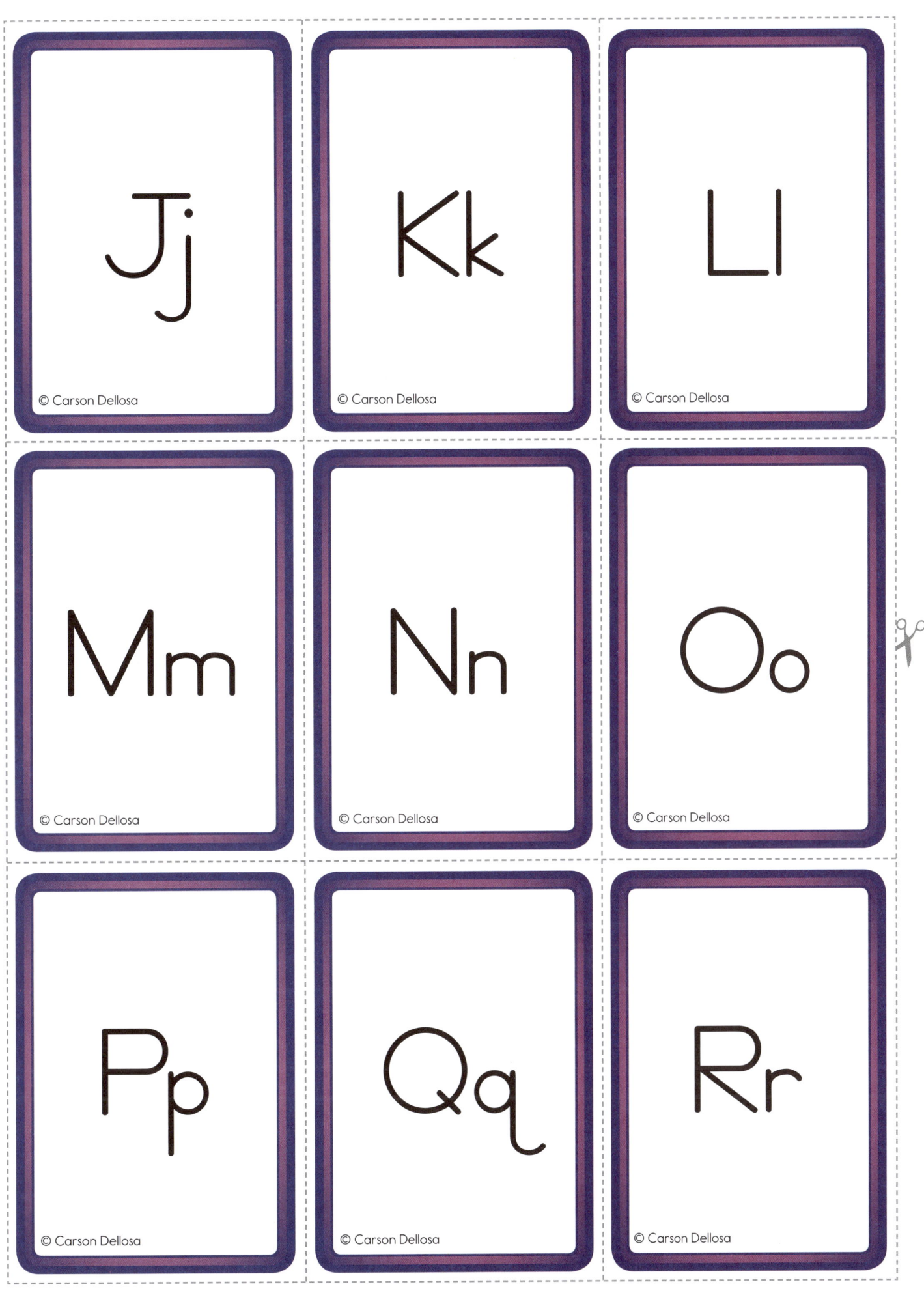

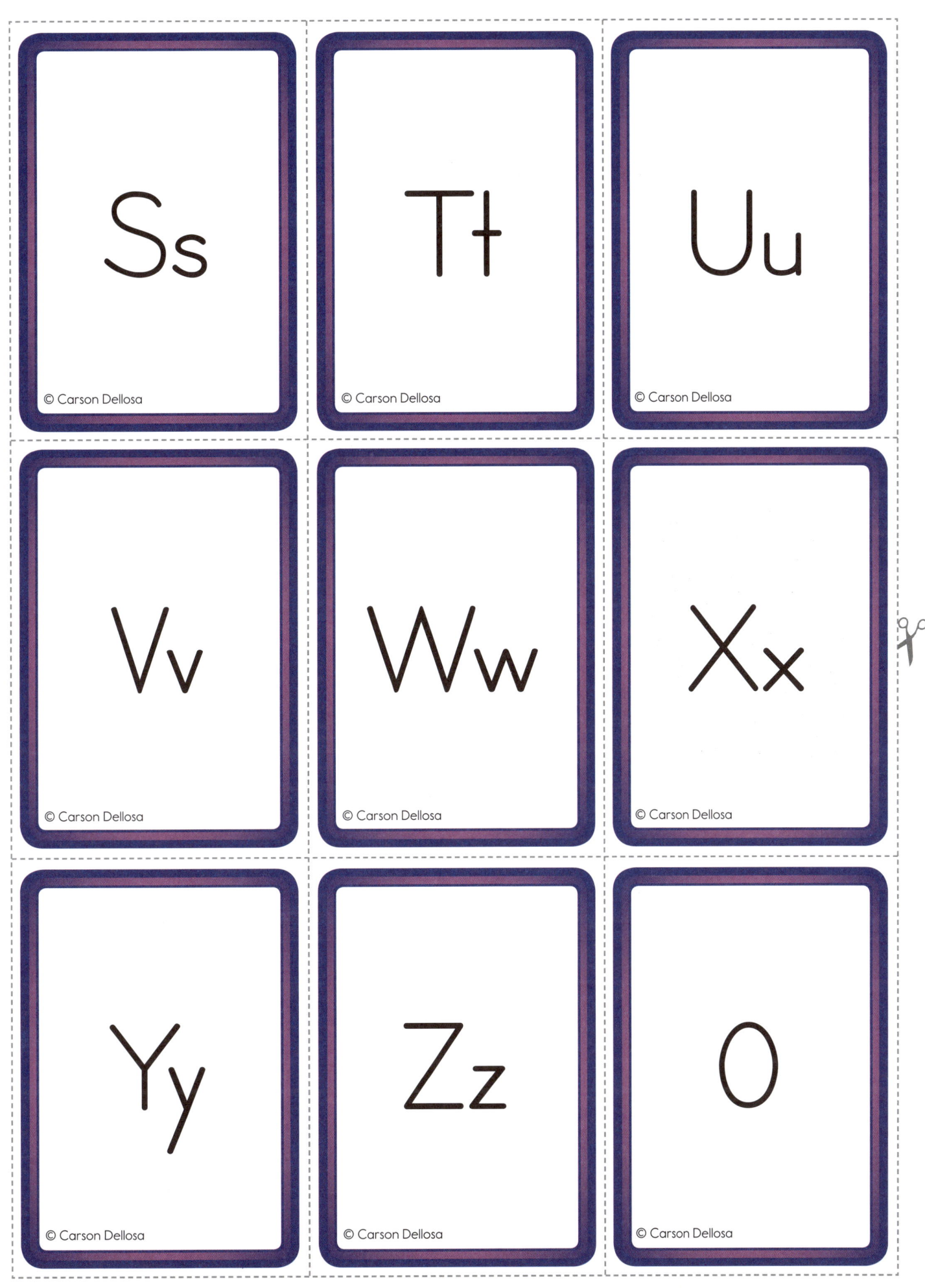

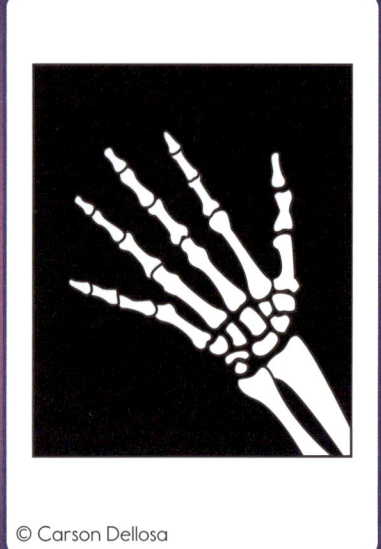

zero

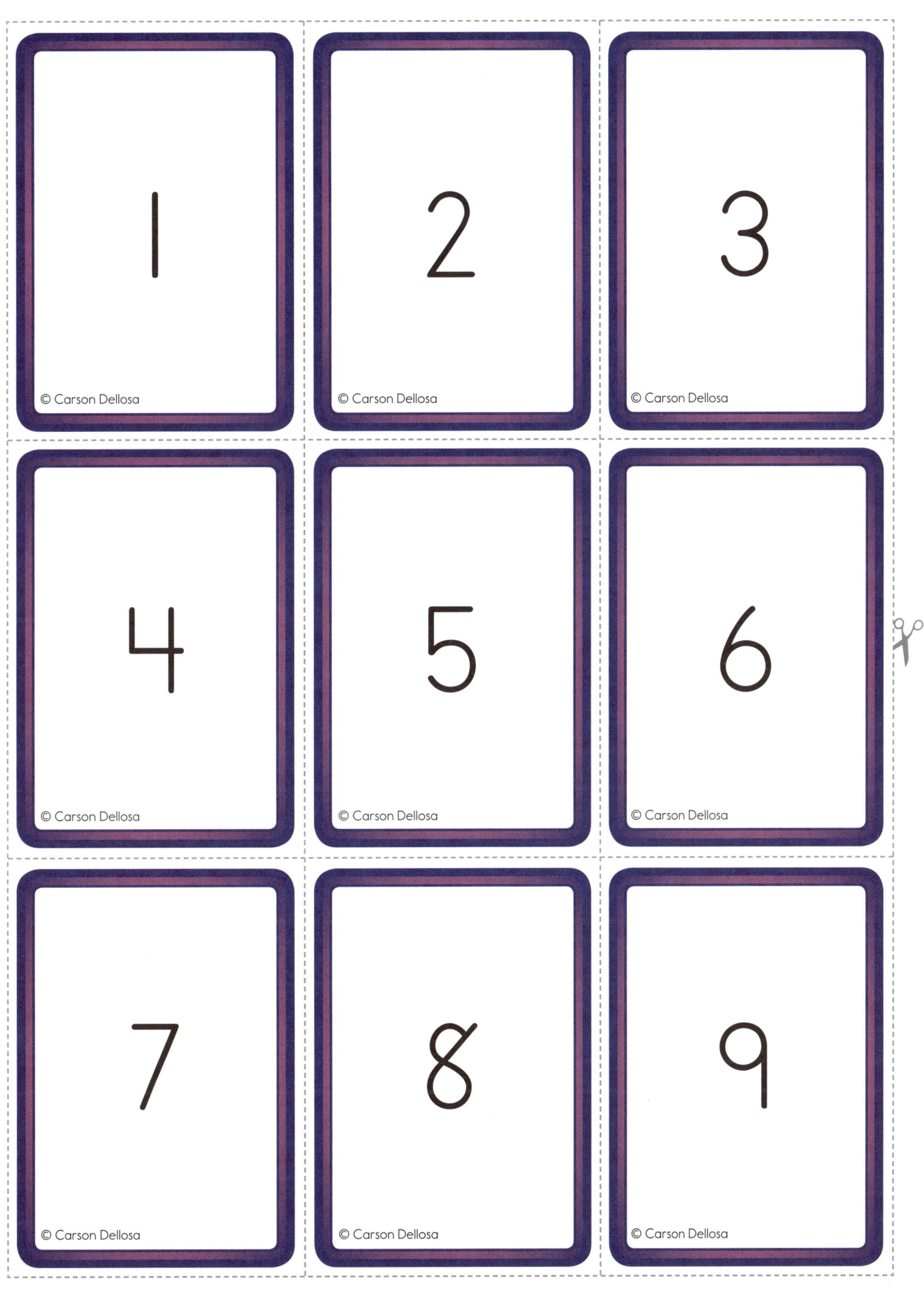

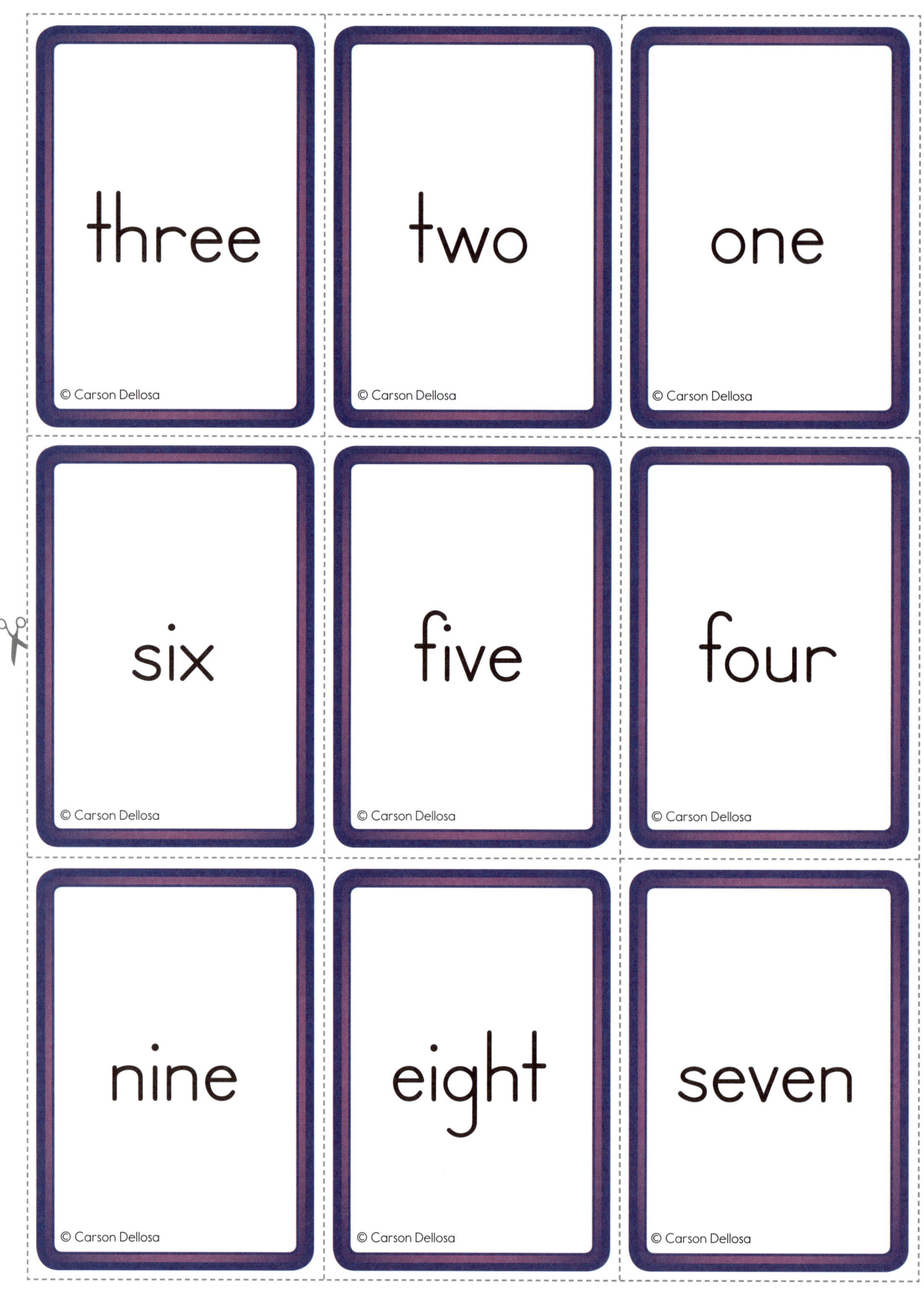

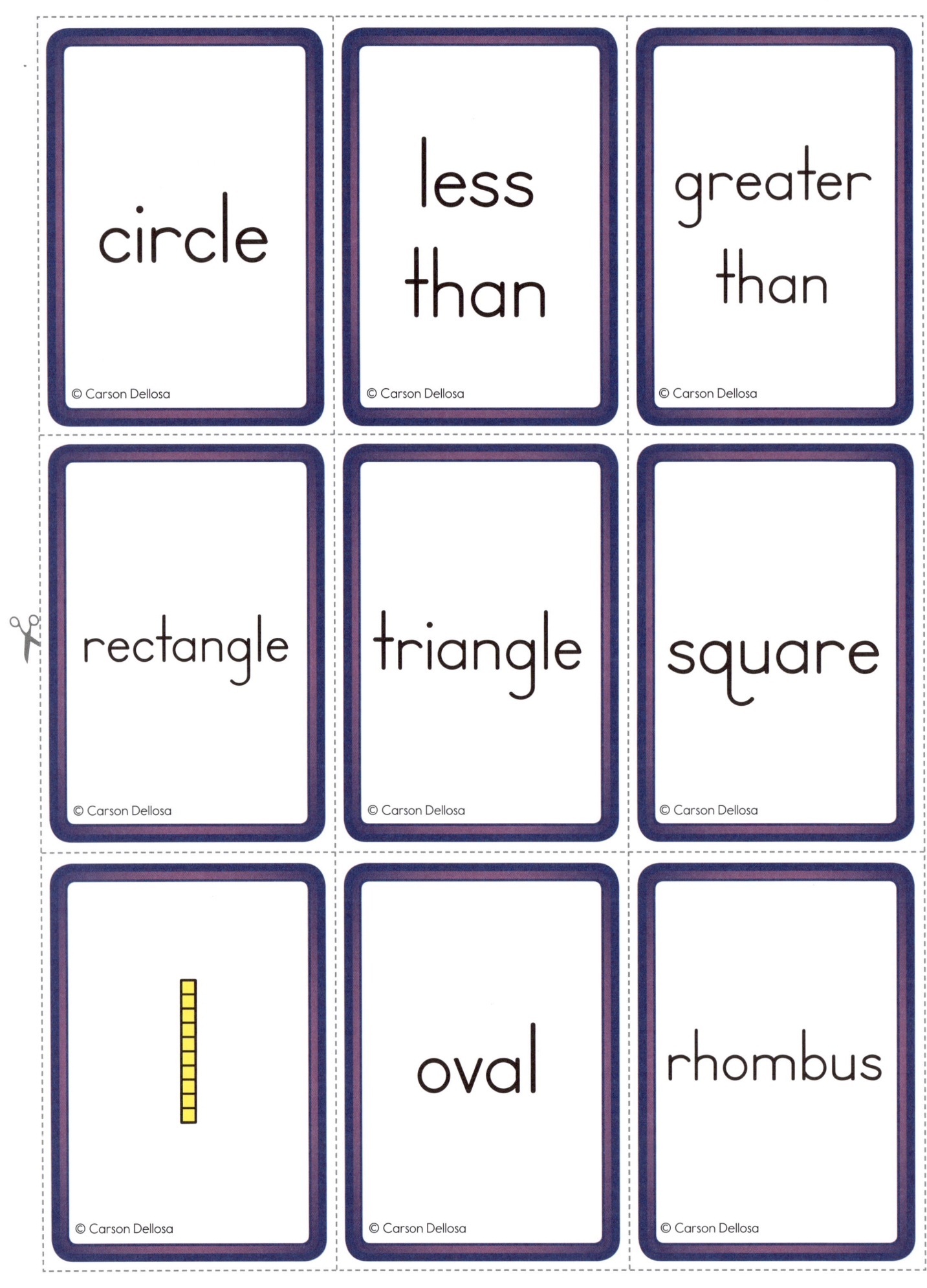

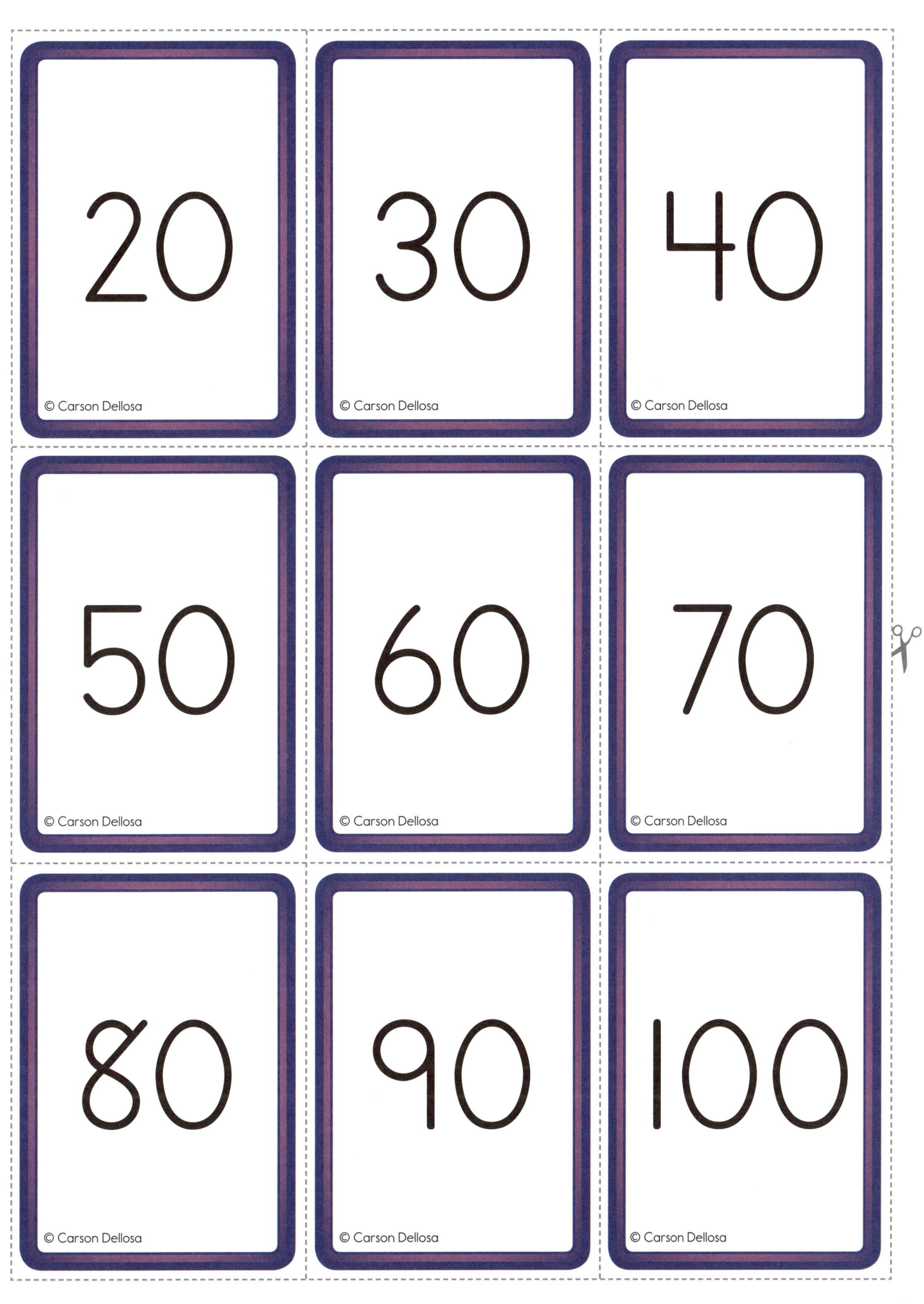

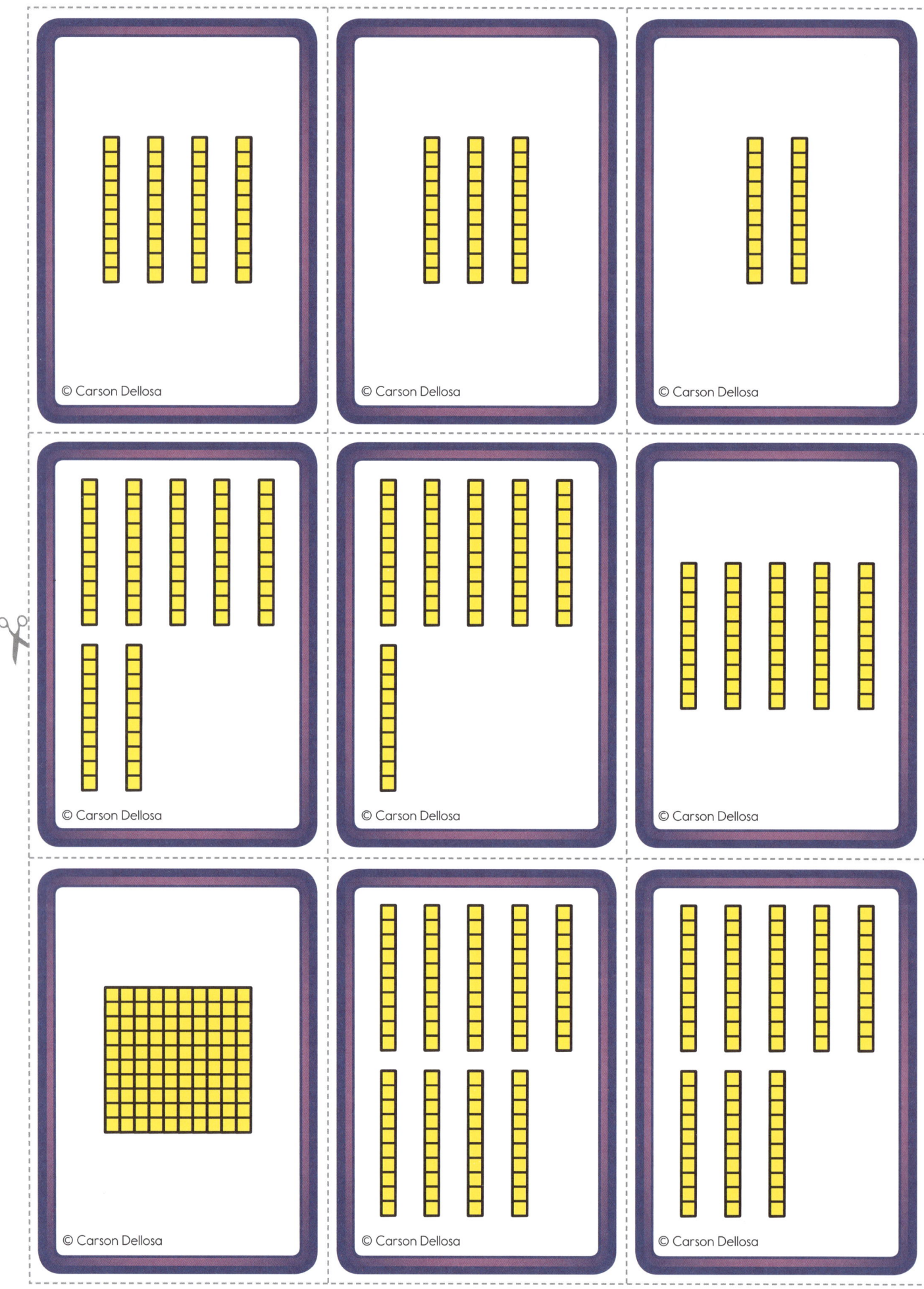